SONGS FROM SHAKESPEARE'S PLAYS
AND POPULAR SONGS OF SHAKESPEARE'S TIME

COMPILED AND EDITED BY

TOM KINES

OAK PUBLICATIONS   NEW YORK, N.Y.
MUSIC SALES LIMITED   LONDON

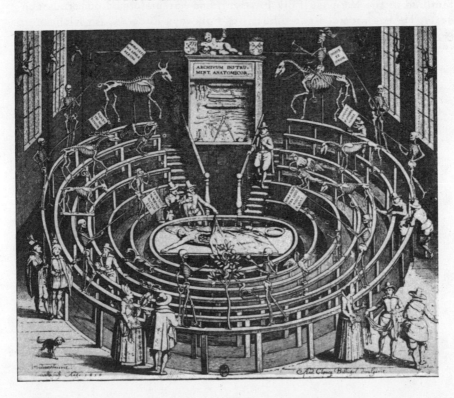

TOM KINES

Photo by Malak

is a singer with a wide range of interests and talents. He began singing at the age of five and has sung leading roles with the Orpheus Operatic Society, the Ottawa Choral Society, the Toronto Bach Society, and the Montreal Bach Choir. As a founding member of the Tudor Singers, he has devoted twelve years to the performance of music of the Elizabethan period, including works for recorder and lute. Mr. Kines has been broadcasting each week for the CBC national radio network in a program called "Song Pedlar." He has done extensive work in television, has been featured at the Mariposa Folk Festival, and has performed numerous concerts. He has recorded two albums for Folkways Records, An Irishman in North Americay (FG 3522) and Popular Songs of Shakespeare's Time (FW 8767).

Cover design by Ronald Clyne
Autography by Carl Rosenthal
Illustrations selected and positioned by Moses Asch
Production Editor Ethel Raim

© Oak Publications, 1964
A Division of Embassy Music Corporation
33 West 60th Street, New York 10023
Music Sales Limited
78 Newman Street, W1 London
Quick Fox Limited
40 Nugget Avenue, Agincourt, Ontario, Canada
Music Sales (Pty.) Limited
27 Clarendon Street, Artarmon, Sydney, NSW, Australia
Printed in the United States

Library of Congress Catalogue #64-66316
ISBN 0-8256-0068-5

CONTENTS

Page

6	Introduction	
9	O mistress mine	*Twelfth Night*
10	Peg o' Ramsey	*Twelfth Night*
11	Three merry men	*Twelfth Night*
12	Hey Robin, Jolly Robin	*Twelfth Night*
13	There dwelt a man in Babylon	*Twelfth Night*
16	Farewell dear love	*Twelfth Night*
18	When that I was a little tiny boy	*Twelfth Night*
20	Titus Andronicus's complaint	*Fortune*
22	Fortune my foe	*Merry Wives*
23	Greensleeves	*Merry Wives of Windsor*
24	To shallow rivers	*Merry Wives*
25	Come live with me and be my love	*Merry Wives*
26	When daffodils begin to peer	*The Winter's Tale*
27	Jog on, jog on the footpath way	*The Winter's Tale*
28	Whoop, do me no harm	*The Winter's Tale*
29	Lawn as white as the driven snow	*The Winter's Tale*
32	How should I your true love know?	*Hamlet*
33	Tomorrow is St. Valentine's Day	*Hamlet*
34	And will he not come again?	*Hamlet*
35	I loathe that I did love	*Hamlet*
36	And let me the canakin clink!	*Othello*
37	King Stephen was a worthy peer	*Othello*
38	Willow song, The	*Othello*
40	Heigh ho for a husband	*Much Ado About Nothing*
42	Sick tune, The	*Much Ado About Nothing*
44	Light o' love	*Two gentlemen of Verona and Much Ado*
46	It was a lover and his lass	*As You Like It*
48	What shall he have that kill'd the deer?	*As You Like It*
49	Hunt is up, The	*Romeo and Juliet*
50	Where griping grief	*Romeo and Juliet*
52	Stephano's songs	*The Tempest*
53	Thou cans't not hit it	*Love's Labour Lost*
54	Come o'er the bourne, Bessy	*King Lear*
56	Calino custurame	*Henry V*
57	Carman's whistle, The	*Henry IV*
58	Fine knacks for ladies	*John Dowland*
60	Since first I saw your face	*Thomas Ford*
62	From the fair Lavinian shore	*John Wilson*
63	Tune thy music to thy heart	*Thomas Campion*
64	Never weather-beaten sail	*Thomas Campion*
66	What if a day	*Thomas Campion*
68	Have you seen but a white lily grow	*Robert Johnson*

(Continued Next Page)

70	Ah! the sighs that come fro' the heart	*William Cornyshe*
71	Pastime with good company	*Henry VIII*
72	Agincourt song, The	
73	Cold's the wind and wet's the rain	*The cobbler's jig*
74	All.in a garden green	*Gathering peascods*
75	Quoth John to Joan	*Wolsey's wild*
76	Who hath his fancy pleas'd	*Wilhelmus van Nassauen*
77	Spanish Lady, The	
78	High Barbary	
81	King Lear and his three daughters	*Flying Fame*
84	When Samson was a tall young man	*Spanish Pavan*
86	Go from my window	
87	Three ravens, The	*Melismata*
88	Of all the birds	*Deuteromelia*
90	Who liveth so merry	*Deuteromelia*
91	Martin said to his man	*Deuteromelia*
92	We be three poor mariners	*Deuteromelia*
93	We be soldiers three	*Deuteromelia*
94	Willy, prithee go to bed	*Deuteromelia*
95	Now Robin lend to me thy bow	*Pammelia*
96	Cryes of London	*Richard Deering*
98	New oysters	*Thomas Ravenscroft*
100	Chairs to mend	*Dr. Hayes*
101	Hey ho! nobody at home	*Pammelia*
102	Loath to depart	*Pammelia*
104	Bibliography	

To the Tudor Singers whose activities led me into
the path of Elizabethan Music and to the other
Ottawa Musicians who helped to make these
wonderful songs come alive again in the 20th
century.

INTRODUCTION

This may not yet be the new Elizabethan age, but certainly there are a lot of amateur poets, musicians and singers who are doing a great deal to enrich their lives and those of their fellowmen with the practise of the arts while contributing their daily stint to industry and commerce.

This book is for them so that they may more easily explore some of the wealth of that other age without the long hours of search and research which have been necessary to produce it.

When Irwin Silber asked me to prepare a book of Shakespeare songs for this quarter-centennial year of the great bard's birth, I thought it was a wonderful idea, for someone else. But as I searched the volumes of reference and the old song books and the list grew, I became more and more excited because I realized that no similar book was available and I knew that when this one was printed, I would be happy to have a copy for my own use!

It is therefore a practical book and I hope a useful book. It has no pretensions to scholarship nor does it attempt to prove anything except that the song-makers of Shakespeare's time were a skilful lot and the combination of the golden flow of poesy with the silver flood of melody and harmony will perhaps never again be equalled.

Naturally, everything excellent of the period could not be included, (there are over 16 volumes in Fellowes' "The English School of Lutenist Song Writers" alone). A degree of selection has been exercised which owes something to the availability, simplicity and authenticity of the material and something to personal preference.

With respect to availability, the latest published volume to present these songs in simple form is the wonderful "Melody and the Lyric" by fellow-Canadian John Murray Gibbon published by Dent in 1930 — now out of print and very scarce. The remaining bibliography as will be seen in the list at the end of the book is mostly older and even harder to acquire. Fortunately, I have been collecting such books for some years.

On the authenticity of the material used I can say only that I have not included without so stating any tune or text that is not of the period. This has of course excluded many beautiful songs; for instance, I very much regret having to exclude "Who is Sylvia" in the magnificent Schubert setting which is so readily adaptable to guitar accompaniment.

Fortunately, Chappell and Co. has just brought out nine of Dr. Arne's beautiful Shakespeare songs and of course Oxford University Press carries the exquisite settings of Peter Warlock as well as many other contemporary composers, thus making most of the good songs from the 18th century onward fairly easy to obtain.

But if we once abandon the restriction of the period contemporary with Shakespeare's life and the lives of those who knew him but survived a few years longer, we would need a book four or five times as large and certainly much more expensive.

I have therefore included only those traditional settings which are believed by scholars to have been in use during Shakespeare's time or have survived in oral tradition.

The New York Public Library has a card file listing over 200 references to songs in Shakespeare's plays — unfortunately, many are lost to us. Either the texts have not survived or the tune is not known or both are missing.

There are other songs important to the plays where music composed at a later period has completely rendered any earlier tunes unacceptable, and some lyrics which simply have no acceptable tunes or known tunes of the period, and some little snatches of songs as given in Caulfield which I did not feel were worth including. To this extent, this book is not a complete collection. Such a collection should be made.

However, it would take a great deal of research to authenticate some of the so-called traditional tunes. Professor Cutts has just published a book — Musique de la Troupe de Shakespeare — but it contains only a few songs from Shakespeare's plays.

J. H. Long of the University of Florida, has tried in his book "Shakespeare's Use of Music" to match up the available texts with contemporary tunes. But this is a very dangerous practise and I cannot accept some of the conclusions he reaches e.g. the manipulation necessary to fit "When daisies pied" or "When icicles hang by the wall" from Love's Labour Lost to "Of all the Birds" from Deuteromelia.

However, this has meant the exclusion of many of the songs appearing in the plays and will no doubt disappoint the amateur directors and producers who may seek them in vain.

May I suggest for the moment at least, it is better to substitute an appropriate song from these pages unless of course the text is Shakespeare's own verse.

The material included consists of (a) songs whose texts were written by Wm. Shakespeare (b) popular songs and ballads quoted or referred to by characters in the plays (c) songs of contemporary poets and musicians (d) popular songs, folk songs, ballads, rounds and street cries, known to have been current at the time and included to add to the overall setting in which Shakespeare wrote and was performed.

I think the rule of simplicity has not been transgressed by the inclusion of 6 lute songs. I feel their inclusion is justified first of all by the quotation of at least two of them in Shakespeare's plays and by the rounded picture of the period which they help to complete. These poet-composers were Shakespeare's contemporaries and some were probably personal friends or acquaintances. Their songs were being collected and published at the same time as his plays and with Ravenscrofts' Pammelia, Deuteromelia and Melismata containing the common popular songs gives us the first comprehensive view of the musical culture of an exciting and bountiful period in the history of music.

Those included here are from among the simplest of accompaniments in the literature and I have further simplified them by giving only the bass notes and chords and transposing them into keys which lie easily under the hand on the guitar.

I am not an instrumentalist and I feel the song must not be subordinate to the accompaniment, so that unless you have a skilled lutenist readily available you should not attempt the lute songs in their original settings.

Many of the chords used will sound strange to modern ears and in some cases I have modified them slightly, and of course no attempt has been made to indicate the position or inversion of the chord.

However, I suggest that you try them this way for a while at least, and I think you will acquire a taste for the sound which is fairly close to the harmony used at the time. The chords should be plucked and/or rolled to give a closer approximation of the lute sound.

Because Elizabethan harmony was often modal and used wonderful mixtures of major and minor, I have indicated a return to a major chord after a predominant use of the minor by the sign (+) e.g. A+ = A Major.

I have also transposed most of the songs which required it, into a medium or low range. Being aware of the wide use of capos among amateur guitarists, I thought it wise to pitch them low so that anyone wanting the pitch raised may apply the capo in the appropriate place.

Finally, then, it is my sincere hope that many amateur singers and guitarists will find a new source of interesting and attractive material in this book and that it will provide them and their friends with many hours of enjoyment.

I wish to acknowledge the very great assistance of the New York Public Library and the British Museum in making books, photostats and microfilms available, and particularly Miss Shepperd of the National Library of Canada for locating important volumes in various universities and other libraries from which they were made available on inter-library loan. Miss Ewart at the Carnegie Library, Ottawa, has been most helpful and very patient with my tendency to keep books overdue, and I want to thank my good friend Wm. France, Mus. Bac. F.C.C.O. for checking the manuscript and harmonies, although I assume full responsibility for what was finally put down.

TOM KINES
Ottawa, Canada
March 1964

O mistress mine

Sung by the clown in "Twelfth Night" Act II Scene III, the tune was arranged by
William Byrd for Queen Elizabeth's Virginal Book of 1611.

O mis—tress mine, where are you roam—ing?

O mis—tress mine, Where are you roam—ing? O stay and hear

your true love's com—ing That can sing both high and low;

Trip — no fur—ther pret—ty sweet—ing; Jour — neys end

in lov—ers' meet—ing, Ev — 'ry wise man's son — doth know.

What is love? tis not hereafter;
Present mirth hath present laughter;
What's to come is still unsure:
In delay there lies no plenty;
Then come kiss me, sweet and twenty,
Youth's a stuff will not endure.

Some call her Peggy and some call her Jean,
And some call her midsummer but they are all
    mista'en,
O Peggy is a bonny lass and works well at the
    mill
For she will be quite occupied while others
    they lie still!

CHORUS

Up goes the hopper and in goes the corn
The wheel it goes about and the stones begin
    to turn.
The meal falls in the meal-trough and quickly
    does it fill,
For Peggy is a bonny lass and works well at
the mill.

Peg o' Ramsay

Shakespeare has Sir Toby Belch refer to this song in "Twelfth Night" Act 2. The verses from Wit and Mirth (1719) exactly fit the tune in Dr. Bull's manuscript book and the less vulgar ones have been used here. The tune ending with the sub dominant chord gives the effect of a round so that the song may continue interminably like many country dance tunes.

Bon — ny Peg-gy Ram — say that a-ny man may see; And bon — ny was her face — with a fair — freck-l'd eye; —

Neat — is her bo — dy made and she hath good skill, And round — are her bon — ny arms that work well at the mill

Bourdon.

With a hey tro-lo-del, hey tro-lo-del, hey tro-lo-del lil; — Bon — ny Peg-gy Ram — say that works well at the

1. 2. mill, With a mill.

Three merry men

Mentioned with other ballads by Sir Toby in Act II Scene 3 of "Twelfth Night".
Chappell says the words to the ballad may be found in Peele's "The Old Wives' Tale"
1595 and the tune in John Playford's M.S. common place book.
Neither Chappell, Long nor Gibbon give more than the four lines:

Three mer — ry men and three mer — ry men and

three mer — ry men _ are we. I in the wood and

thou on the ground and Jack sleeps in _ the tree.

1. Hold thy peace, and I prith — ee hold thy peace,

2. Thou knave Hold thy peace thou knave,

3. thou knave.

Hey Robin, jolly Robin

In Act IV Scene 2 of "Twelfth Night" Feste the clown baits Malvolio with a quote from Sir Thomas Wyatt's (1503–1542) poem which was set by Wm. Cornyshe during the reign of Henry VIII. The complete song in three parts is in Noah Greenberg's English Song Book, but uses only two verses of the poem as given in Percy.

Hey Ro—bin, Jol—ly Ro—bin, tell me how thy La—dy does.

Hey Ro—bin, Jol—ly Ro—bin, tell me how thy La—dy does.

A Robin, jolly Robin,
Tell me how thy leman doeth,
And thou shalt know of mine.

My lady is unkind perde,
Alack, why is she so?
She loveth another better than me,
And yet she will say no.

I find no such doubleness,
I find women true;
My lady loveth me doubtless,
And will change for no new.

Thou art happy while that doth last;
But I say as I find,
That women's love is but a blast
And turneth with the wind.

There dwelt a man in Babylon

One of the songs quoted briefly by Sir Toby in Act II Scene 3 of "Twelfth Night". It is the beginning of a broadside called "The Ballad of Constant Susannah" given in Pepys Vol. I p. 33. The tune as given by Naylor (1896).

There dwelt a man in Babylon,
    Of reputation great by fame;
He took to wife a fair woman,
    Susanna she was called by name;
A woman fair and virtuous,
    Lady, Lady,
Why should we not of her learn thus
    To live godly?

Virtuously her life she led,
    She feared God, she stood in awe,
As in the stories we have read,
    Was well brought up in Moses' law.
Her parents they were godly folk,
    Lady, Lady,
Why should we not then sing and talk
    Of this Lady?

That year two judges there was made,
    Which were the Elders of Babylon;
To Joachim's house was all their trade,
    Who was Susanna's husband then;
Joachim was a great rich man,
    Lady, Lady,
These elders oft to his house came
    For this Lady.

Joachim had an orchard by,
    Fast joining to his house or place,
Whereas Susanna commonly
    Herself did daily there solace;
And that these elders soon espied,
    Lady, Lady
And privily themselves did hide
    For that Lady.

Her chaste and constant life was tried
   By these two elders of Babylon;
A time conveniently they espied
   To have this lady all alone.
In his orchard it came to pass,
   Lady, Lady,
Where she alone herself did wash
   Her fair body.

These elders came to her anon,
   And thus they said, "Fair dame, God speed,
Thy doors are fast, thy maids are gone,
   Consent to us and do this deed;
For we are men of no mistrust,
   Lady, Lady,
And yet to thee we have a lust,
   O fair Lady!"

If that to us thou dost say nay,
   A testimonial we will bring;
We will say that one with thee lay,
   How cans't thou then avoid the thing?
Therefore consent, and to us turn,
   Lady, Lady,
For we to thee in lust do burn,
   O fair Lady."

Then did she sigh and said, "Alas,
   Now woe is me on every side;
Was ever wretch in such a case,
   Shall I consent and do this deed?
Whether I do it or do it not,"
   Lady, Lady,
"It is my death, right well I wot,"
   O true Lady!

"Better it were for me to fall
   Into your hands this day guiltless,
Than that I should consent at all
   To this your shameful wickedness."
And even with that (whereas she stood)
   Lady, Lady,
Unto the Lord she cried aloud —
   Pitifully.

These elders both likewise again
   Against Susanna aloud they cried,
Their filthy lust could not obtain,
   Their wickedness they sought to hide;
Unto her friends they then her brought,
   Lady, Lady,
And with all speed the life they sought
   Of that Lady.

On the morrow she was brought forth
   Before the people there to stand,
That they might hear and know the truth,
   How these two elders Susanna found.
The elders swore and thus did say,
   Lady, Lady,
How that they saw a young man lay
   With that Lady.

Judgement there was, for no offence,
   Susanna causeless then must die;
These elders bore such evidence,
   Against her they did verify.
Who were believ-ed then indeed,
   Lady, Lady,
Against Susanna to proceed,
   That she should die.

Susanna's friends that stood her by,
   They did lament, and were full woe,
When as they saw no remedy
   But that to death she then must go.
(....................................)
   Lady, Lady,
In God was all her hope and trust,
   To Him did cry.

The Lord her voice heard and beheld
   The daughter's cry of Israel;
His spirit he raised in a child,
   Whose name was call-ed young Daniel,
Who cried aloud whereas he stood,
   Lady, Lady,
I am clear of the guiltless blood
   Of this Lady.

"Are you such fools?" quoth Daniel then;
   "In judgement you have not done well,
Nor yet the right way have you gone
   To judge a daughter of Israel.
By this witness of false disdain;
   Lady, Lady
Wherefore to judgement turn again
   For that Lady."

And when to judgement they were set,
   He call-ed for those wicked men,
And soon he did them separate,
   Putting the one from the other, then
He asked the first where he did see
   That fair Lady;
He said — under a mulberry tree;
   Who lied falsely.

"Thou liest," said Daniel, "on thy head
    Thy sentence is before the Lord!"
He bade that forth he might be led,
    And bring the other that bore record;
To see how they two did agree
    For this Lady,
He said — under a Pomgrannat tree;
    Who lied falsely.

Said Daniel as he did before,
    "Behold the messenger of the Lord
Stands waiting for you at the door,
    Even to cut thee with a sword!"
And even with that, the multitude
    Aloud did cry,
"Give thanks to God!" so to conclude
    For this Lady.

They dealt like with these wicked men
    According as the scripture saith,
They did, as with their neighbour then
    By Moses' law were put to death!
The innocent preserv-ed was,
    Lady, Lady,
As God by Daniel brought to pass
    For this Lady.

        Finis

Farewell, dear love

In "Twelfth Night" Act II Scene 3 after Sir Toby has quoted from several of the songs given here, Malvolio enters to put an end to the revel. His last word "farewell" starts Sir Toby on another song which turns out to be Robert Jones' "Farewell dear love". The version in the play is a little garbled but Naylor shows how it can be matched to the tune. The song is given here from Robert Jones' "First Book of Songs and Ayres" (1600).

Fare – well dear love, since thou wilt needs be gone,

mine eyes do show my life is al – most gone.

Nay I will ne – ver die so long as I can spy.

There be ma—ny mo' tho' that she do

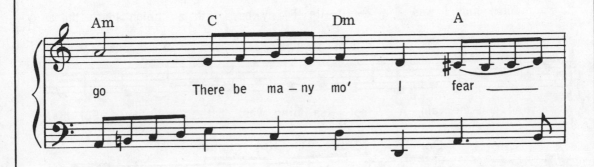

go There be ma—ny mo' I fear _____

not, Why then _ let her go, I care not.

Farewell, farewell, since this I find is true,
I will not spend more time in wooing you;
But I will seek elsewhere, if I may find love
    there.
Shall I bid her go? What and if I do?
Shall I bid her go and spare not?
Oh no, no, no, I dare not!

Ten thousand time's farewell; — yet stay
    awhile: —
Sweet, kiss me once; sweet kisses time beguile.
I have no pow'r to move. How now am I in love?
Wilt thou needs begone: Go then, all is one.
Wilt thou needs begone: Oh, hie thee!
Nay stay, and do no more deny me.

Once more adieu, I see loath to depart
Bids oft adieu to her, that holds my heart.
But seeing I must lose thy love, which I did
    choose,
Go thy way for me, since that may not be.
Go, thy ways for me. But whither?
Go, of but where I may come thither.

What shall I do? My love is now departed.
She is as fair, as she is cruel-hearted.
She would not be entreated, with prayers
    oft repeated;
If she come no more, shall I die therefore?
If she come no more, what care I?
Faith let her go, or come, or tarry!

When that I was a little tiny boy

This song is in the epilogue of "Twelfth Night" and the tune is believed by most authorities to be the traditional one to which it was sung in Shakespeare's day.

But when I came to man's estate,
With a heigh! ho! the wind and the rain,
'Gainst thieves and knaves men shut their gate,
For the rain it raineth ev'ry day.

CHORUS

But when I came, alas! to wive,
With a heigh! ho! the wind and the rain,
By swaggering never could I thrive,
For the rain it raineth ev'ry day.

CHORUS

A great while ago the world begun,
With a heigh! ho! the wind and the rain,
But that's all one, our play is done,
And we'll strive to please you every day.

GOOD FREND FOR IESVS SAKE FORBEARE,
TO DIGG THE DVST ENCLOASED HEARE:
BLEST BE Y MAN Y SPARES THES STONES,
AND CVRST BE HE Y MOVES MY BONES

Mr. WILLIAM

SHAKESPEARES

COMEDIES,
HISTORIES, &
TRAGEDIES.

Published according to the True Originall Copies.

LONDON
Printed by Isaac Iaggard, and Ed. Blount. 1623

Titus Andronicus's complaint

In Percy's "Reliques", the author makes a case for this ballad providing the inspiration for Shakespeare's play "Titus Andronicus" although they differ in many details. As the ballad was intended to be sung to the tune "Fortune" the text is given hereunder for those who wish to combine the two.

You noble minds, and famous martiall wights,
That in defence of native country fights,
Give care to me, tat ten yeeres fought for
    Rome,
Yet reapt disgrace at my returning home.

In Rome I lived in fame fulle threescore yeeres,
My name beloved was of all my peeres;
Full five-and-twenty valiant sonnes I had,
Whose forwarde vertues made their father glad.

For when Romes foes their warlike forces bent,
Against them stile my sonnes and I were sent;
Against the Goths full ten yeeres weary warre
We spent, receiving many a bloudy scarre.

Just two-and-twenty of my sonnes were slaine
Before we did returne to Rome againe:
Of five-and-twenty sonnes, I brought but three
Alive, the stately towers of Rome to see.

When wars were done, I conquest home did
    bring,
And did present my prisoners to the king,
The Queene of Goths, her sons, and eke a
    Moore,
Which did such murders, like was nere before.

The emperour did make this queene his wife,
Which bred in Rome debate and deadlie strife;
The Moore, with her two sonnes, did groe soe
    proud,
That none like them in Rome might bee allowd.

The Moore soe pleas'd this new-made empress'
    eie,
That she consented to him secretlye
For to abuse her husbands marriage-bed,
And soe in time a blackamore she bred.

Then she, whose thoughts to murder were
    inclinde,
Consented with the Moore of bloody minde
Against myselfe, my kin, and all my friendes,
In cruell sort to bring them to their endes.

Soe when in age I thought to live in peace,
Both care and griefe began then to increase:
Amongst my sonnes I had one daughter bright,
Which joy'd and pleased best my aged sight.

My deare Lavinia was betrothed than
To Cesars sonne, a young and noble man:
Who, in a hunting by the emperours wife
And her two sonnes, bereaved was of life.

He, being slaine, was cast in cruel wise
Into a darksome den from light of skies:
The cruell Moore did come that way as then
With my three sonnes, who fell into the den.

The Moore then fecht the emperour with speed,
For to accuse them of that murderous deed;
And when my sonnes within the den were found,
In wrongfull prison they were cast and bound.

But nowe behold what wounded most my mind:
The empresses two sonnes, of savage kind,
My daughter ravished without remorse,
And took away her honour, quite perforce.

When they had tasted of soe sweete a flowre,
Fearing this sweete should shortly turn to sowre,
They cutt her tongue, whereby she could not tell
How that dishonoure unto her befell.

Then both her hands they basely cutt of quite,
Whereby their wickednesse she could not write,
Nor with her needle on her sampler sowe
The bloudye workers of her direfull woe.

My brother Marcus found her in the wood,
Staining the grassie ground with purple bloud,
That trickled from her stumpes and bloudlesse
    armes:
Noe tongue at all she had to tell her harmes.

But when I saw her in that woefull case,
With teares of bloud I wet mine aged face:
For my Lavinia I lamented more
Then for my two-and twenty sonnes before.

When as I sawe she could not write nor speake,
With grief mine aged heart began to breake;
We spred an heape of sand upon the ground,
Whereby those bloudy tyrants out we found.

For with a staffe, without the helpe of hand,
She writt these wordes upon the plat of sand:
"The lustfull sonnes of the proud emperésse
Are doers of this hateful wickednésse."

I tore the milk-white hairs from off mine head,
I curst the houre wherein I first was bred;
I wisht this hand, that fought for countrie's
    fame,
In cradle rockt, had first been stroken lame.

The Moore, delighting still in villainy,
Did say, to sett my sonnes from prison free,
I should unto the king my right hand give,
And then my three imprisoned sonnes should
    live.

The Moore I caus'd to strike it off with speede,
Whereat I grieved not to see it bleed,
But for my sonnes would willingly impart,
And for their ransome send my bleeding heart.

But as my life did linger thus in paine,
They sent to me my bootlesse hand againe,
And therewithal the heades of my three sonnes,
Which filld my dying heart with fresher moanes.

Then, past reliefe, I upp and downe did goe,
And with my teares writ in the dust my woe:
I shot my arrowes towards heaven hie,
And for revenge to hell often did crye.

The empresse then, thinking that I was mad,
Like Furies she and both her sonnes were clad,
(She nam'd Revenge, and Rape and Murder they)
To undermine and heare what I would say.

I fed their foolish veines a certaine space,
Until my friendes did find a secret place,
Where both her sonnes unto a post were bound,
And just revenge in cruell sort was found.

I cut their throates, my daughter held the pan
Betwixt her stumpes, wherein the bloud it ran:
And then I ground their bones to powder small,
And made a paste for pyes streight therewithhall.

Then with their fleshe I made two mighty pyes,
And at a banquet served in stately wise,
Before the empresse set this loathsome meat;
So of her sonnes own fleshe she well did eat.

Myselfe bereav'd my daughter then of life,
The empresse then I slewe with bloudy knife,
And stabb'd the emperour immediatelie,
And then myself: even soe did Titus die.

Then this revenge against the Moore was found:
Alive they sett him halfe into the ground,
Whereas he stood until such time he starv'd:
And soe God send all murderers may be serv'd.

Fortune my foe

There is a reference to this song in "The Merry Wives of Windsor", Act III, Scene 3, where Falstaff says, "I see what thou wert, if Fortune thy foe were not, Nature thy friend."
The air appears in a setting by Wm. Byrd in The Fitzwilliam Virginal Book which places it between 1550 and 1620.

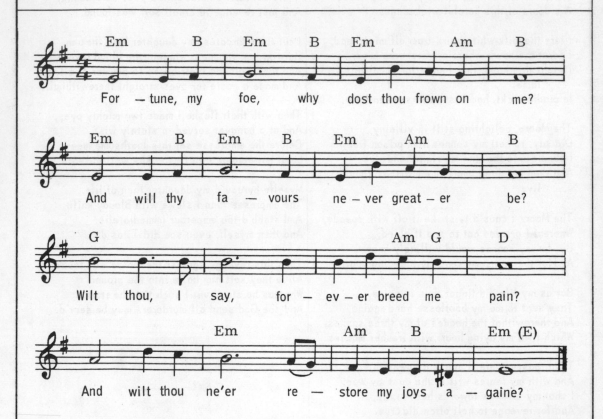

For — tune, my foe, why dost thou frown on me?

And will thy fa — vours ne — ver great — er be?

Wilt thou, I say, for — ev — er breed me pain?

And wilt thou ne'er re — store my joys a — gaine?

Fortune hath wrought me grief and great annoy;
Fortune hath falsely stolen my love away.
My love and joy whose sight did make me glad;
Such great misfortunes never young man had.

Greensleeves

This song is undoubtedly the most popular song of the period surviving to the present day. Shakespeare mentioned it twice in "Merry Wives" — Act II Scene I and in Act V Scene V. The tune is in W. Ballet's Lute Book but the ballad is noted in the Stationers' Register for September 1580.

A — las, my love, you do me wrong to cast me off dis-

cour-teous-ly, And I have lov-ed you so long, de-

light-ing in your com-pa-ny. Green-sleeves was all my joy,

Green-sleeves was my de-light, Green-sleeves was my

heart of gold, And who but my La-dy Green-sleeves.

I have been ready at your hand
To grant whatever you would crave;
I have both wagered life and land,
Your love and good will for to have.

CHORUS

Thou couldst desire no earthly thing,
But still thou hadst it readily;
Thy music still to play and sing
And yet thou wouldst not love me.

CHORUS

Well, I will pray to God on high
That thou constancy mayest see,
And that yet once before I die,
Thou wilt vouchsafe to love me.

To shallow rivers

Bridge says "tune anonymous, date probably 16th century." This poor tune is certainly no more than a corrupt form of "Walsingham". The right tune is that of "Come Live With Me," which follows. I think this one is more interesting, probably later, and certainly a more sophisticated air for a serenade. You'll find this version sung by the Welsh parson in "Merry Wives of Windsor", Act III, Scene 1.

To shal – low riv – ers __ to whose falls Mel – od – ious
birds __ sing __ mad – ri – gals. There will we make our beds of
ros – es, And __ a thous – and fra – grant pos – ies.

Come live with me and be my love

Izaac Walton is quoted as authority for claiming Christopher Marlowe as the author of this song, but the verses appear in shortened form in Shakespeare's "Sonnet to sundry notes of music" and parts of verses 2 and 3 are quoted in "The Merry Wives of Windsor", Act III, Scene 1. The tune is from W. Corkine's "Second book of Ayres", 1612.

Come live with me and be my love,
And we will all ____ the treas — ures prove. That
hills and val — leys, dale and field,
And all the crag — gy moun — tains yield.

*A folk song using some of these words may be found in Marjorie Kennedy Fraser's "Songs of the Hebrides" under the title "A Clyde-side love lilt".

There will we sit upon the rocks
And see the shepherds feed their flocks,
By shallow rivers to whose falls
Melodious birds sing madrigals.

There will I make thee beds of roses
And a thousand fragrant posies,
A cap of flowers and a kirtle
Embroider'd all with leaves of myrtle.

A gown made of the finest wool,
Which from our pretty lambs we'll pull;
Fair lined slippers for the cold,
With buckles of the purest gold.

A belt of straw and ivy buds
With coral clasps and amber studs;
And if these pleasures may thee move,
Come live with me and be my love.

The shepherd swains shall dance and sing
For thy delight each May morning;
If these delights thy mind may move,
Then live with me and be my love.

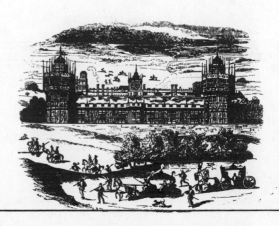

When daffodils begin to peer

This is the first song sung by Autolycus, Shakespeare's only representation of a genuine ballad-monger. It appears in "The Winter's Tale", Act IV, Scene 3. The tune given without identification in Caulfield is attributed by Baring-Gould to Dr. Boyce (1710–1719).

I have used the tune given for the first verse for both it and the second but as it is a through-composed song with a rather unsatisfactory ending, I have taken the liberty of revising the last verse.

1. When daf — fo — dils be — gin to peer, With heigh the dox — y ov — er the dale; Why then comes in the sweet o the year for the red blood runs in the win — ter's pale.

3. The lark that tir — ra tir — ra chants with hey, with hey, the thrush and the jay, Are sum — mer songs for me and my aunts while we lie tumb — ling in the hay.

2. The white sheet bleaching on the hedge,
With heigh! the sweet birds, O, how they
    sing!
Doth set my pugging tooth an edge,
For a quart of ale is a dish for a king.

Jog on, jog on the footpath way

Autolycus makes his exit in Act IV, Scene 3 of "The Winter's Tale" with one stanza of this song which appeared in "The Antidote against Melancholy" 1661 to the tune of 'Hanskin.' It has also appeared in many other 17th century song books, attesting to its popularity at the time.

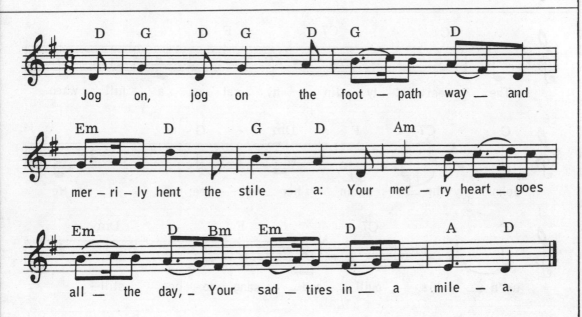

Jog on, jog on the foot — path way — and mer — ri — ly hent the stile — a: Your mer — ry heart — goes all — the day, — Your sad — tires in — a mile — a.

Cast care away, let sorrow cease,
A fig for melancholy;
Let's laugh and sing, or, if you please,
We'll frolic with sweet Dolly.

Your paltry money-bags of gold,
What need have we to stare for?
When little or nothing soon is told,
And we have the less to care for.

The lark that lirra-lirra chants,
With heigh, with heigh, the thrush and the jay,
Are summer songs for me and my aunts,
While we lie tumbling in the hay.

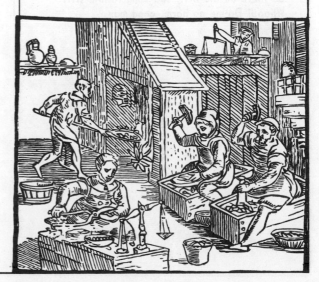

Whoop, do me no harm

Twice mentioned in Act IV, Scene 3 of "The Winter's Tale" in the servant's description of Autolycus's Repertoire. Chappell gives a tune from Corkine's "First Book of Ayres" but the tune used here is the one quoted by Sir Frederick Bridge from a 17th century viol da gamba book. The words are from Westminster Drollery (1672).

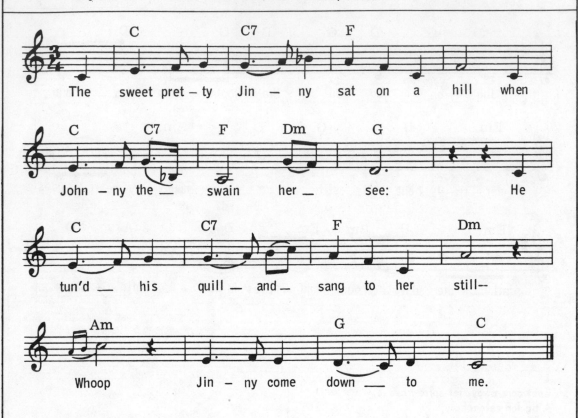

The sweet pret-ty Jin — ny sat on a hill when
John — ny the — swain her — see: He
tun'd — his quill — and — sang to her still—
Whoop Jin — ny come down — to me.

But she sang, but she sang, but she sang to him,
O do ye no harm to me.
So there on the hill, she sang to him still
Whoop! Do me no harm, good man.

28

Lawn as white as the driven snow

After the servant's description of his powers in Act IV Scene 4 of the Winter's Tale, Autolycus enters singing his pedlar's song. It is generally attributed to Dr. John Wilson who is believed to be the boy singer "Jackie Wilson" appearing in the original cast of Much Ado". It was not published however until 1660 in his "Cheerful Ayres or Ballads" when he was a Mus. Doc. Oxon., a professor at the university and Gentleman of the Chapel Royal.

head to heel ____ What maids _ lack _ from head _ to heel ____

_ Come buy of me, ─ Come. Come _ buy, _ come _

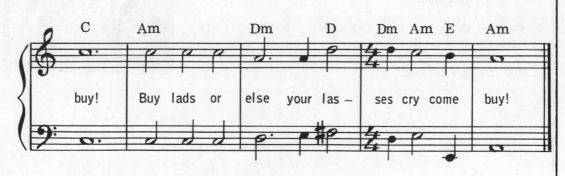

buy! Buy lads or else your las ─ ses cry come buy!

How should I your true love know

The first of Ophelia's "Mad Songs" from Act IV, Scene 5 of "Hamlet". The tune is traditional as given by Hullah.

How should I your — true love know From an-oth-er one?

By his cock-le — hat and staff, And his sand-al shoon.

He is dead and gone, lady,
He is dead and gone;
At his head a grass-green turf
At his heels a stone.

White his shroud as the mountain snow.
Larded with sweet flowers,
Which bewept to the grave did not .go,
With true-love showers.

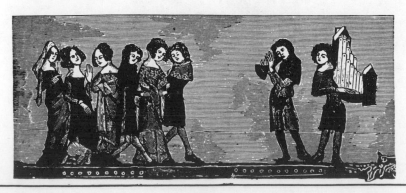

Tomorrow is St. Valentine's day

Tune "Who list to lead a soldier's life" mentioned by Peele in his Edward III (1593). The traditional tune has survived and been used for several songs. It remains one of the most charming, simple melodies in English balladry.

In "Hamlet" Act IV, Scene 5, Ophelia, her hair hanging down, sings and plays upon a lute:

To-morr-row is _ St. Val-en-tine's day all in _ the morn-ing

time. _ And I _ a maid _ at your win-dow to

be _ your Val-en-tine. _

Then up he rose and down'd his clothes
And dupp'd the chamber door,
Let in a maid that out a maid
Never departed more.

By Gis and by Saint Charity
Alack and fie for shame!
Young men will do't if they come to 't;
By cock, they are to blame.

Quoth she, "Before you tumbled me,
You promis'd me to wed:"
"So would I ha' done, by yonder sun,
An thou hads't not come to my bed."

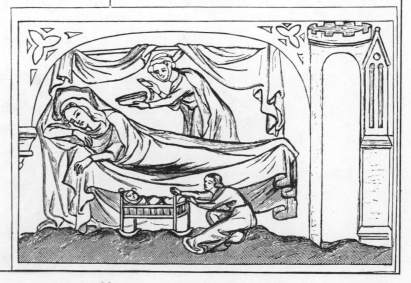

And will he not come again

Claimed by Hullah to have been preserved by the traditions of the stage, this beautifully plaintive little melody to which Ophelia sings the last of her "mad songs" in Act
IV, Scene 5 of "Hamlet" is worthy of a much longer song.

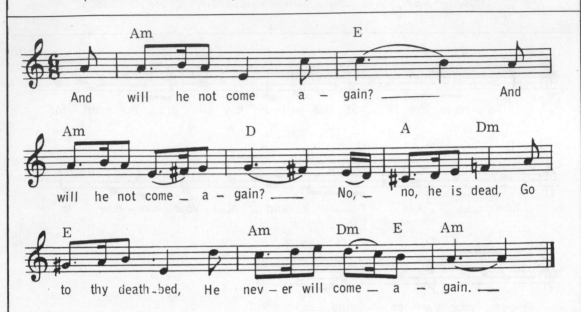

And will he not come a — gain? _____ And
will he not come _ a — gain? ____ No, _ no, he is dead, Go
to thy death _ bed, He nev — er will come _ a — gain. ___

His beard was as white as snow,
All flaxen was his poll;
He is gone, he is gone,
And we cast away moan:
God'a' mercy on his soul.

G.T.Sargent. sc.

I loath that I did love

The famous grave-digger's song in Act V Scene 1 of "Hamlet" is a garbled version of a poem attributed to Thomas Lord Vaux, published in 1557. Jackson gives the whole song with what may be the original air, but it has been traditionally sung to the tune "Now Ponder Well" or "The Children in the Wood".

I loathe that I did love, did love, In youth that I thought sweet: As time re – quires for my be – hove, Me – thinks they are not meet.

The original words are:

In youth when I did love,
Me thought 'twas very sweet;
As time requires for my belove,
Methinks it is not meet.

For age with stealing steps
Hath clawed me in his clutch;
And lusty youth away he leaps,
As there had been none such.

A pick-axe and a spade,
And eke a shrouding sheet,
A home of clay for to be made
For such a guest most meet.

And let me the canakin clink

Caulfield gives what is assumed to be the traditional tune, but characteristically has nothing to say about its source. In Act II Scene 3 of "Othello", Iago uses the song to induce Cassio to drink.

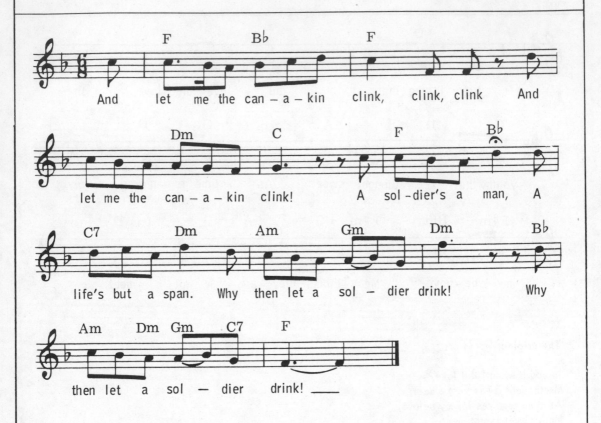

And let me the can — a — kin clink, clink, clink And let me the can — a — kin clink! A sol — dier's a man, A life's but a span. Why then let a sol — dier drink! Why then let a sol — dier drink! ___

King Stephen was a worthy peer

Iago's second song ("Othello" Act II Scene 3) is part of an old ballad relating to the stinginess of the 12th Century King of England (1135—1154). This "traditional tune" is as given in Caulfield, again with no information as to source. Gibbon gives a tune from Chambers' "Scottish Song" which Allan Ramsay ascribed to the old Scots song "Take Thine Auld Cloak About Ye". See also Percy, Vol. 1, p. 139, for another text.

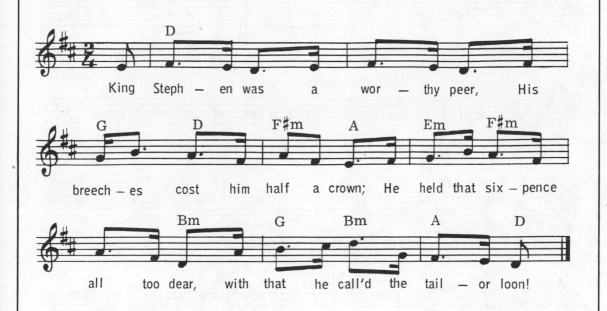

King Steph — en was a wor — thy peer, His breech — es cost him half a crown; He held that six — pence all too dear, with that he call'd the tail — or loon!

He was a wight of high renown,
And thou art but of low degree:
'Tis pride that pulls the country down;
Then tak' thine auld clock about thee.

Willow song, The

Perhaps the most famous and certainly one of the most beautiful songs used in Shakespeare's plays, "Willow, Willow" occurs in "Othello" Act IV Scene III where it is sung by Desdemona prior to her death at the hands of Othello. The earliest copy of the music is in a lute book dated 1583 in the Library of Trinity College, Dublin.

The fresh streams ran by her, and murmer'd her
    moans;
Sing willow, willow, willow;
Her salt tears fell from her and soft'ned the
    stones;

Let nobody blame him, his scorn I approve
Sing willow, willow, willow,
He was born to be fair, I to die for his love.*

CHORUS

I call'd my love false love, but what said he
    then?
Sing willow, willow, willow
If I court more women, you'll couch with
    more men.

*I have supplied the missing line from a 25-stanza
version in the Pepys collection (Percy P. 142) on
which Shakespeare is said to have based his song.

Heigh ho for a husband

Mentioned twice in "Much Ado About Nothing" Act III Scenes I and IV, the words are in the Pepsyian Collection and in "Wit and Mirth". The tune is in John Gamble's Manuscript Common Place Book.

There was a maid the oth—er day Sigh—ed sore, "God wot!" And she said, "All wives might have their way but __ maid—ens they might not. Full eight—een years have pass'd," she said, "since I poor soul was born, And if I __ chance to __ die __ a __ maid, A—pol—lo is fore— sworn. Heigh — ho! _____ for a hus—band Heigh — ho! _____ __ for a hus—band," Still this was __ her __ song. "I will have a __

hus – band, have _ a hus – band be ___ he old or young."

An ancient suitor to her came.
His beard was almost grey;
Tho' he was old and she was young,
She would no longer stay.
But to her mother went this maid,
And told her by and by,
That she a husband needs must have
And this was still her cry:

CHORUS

"A wedded life, ah! well-a-day,
It is a hapless lot!
Young maids may marry, be they gay,
Young wives, alas, may not!
A twelve-month is too long to bear
This sorry yoke," she said,
"Since wives they may not have their will,
'Tis best to die a maid!

Heigh-ho! with a husband, Heigh-ho! with a
husband,
What a life lead I!
Out upon a husband, such a husband,
Fie, fie, fie, Oh! fie!"

Sick tune, The

In "Much Ado About Nothing" Act III Scene 5, Hero says, "Why, how now! do you speak in the _sick tune_?" and Beatrice answers, "I am out of all other tune, methinks". The tune as given is from the "Cittharn School" 1597. The text is from a ballad in Ritson's "Ancient Songs" based on the massacre of a lady and her household, 37 persons in all, by the Captain Care named in the first stanza. Several versions are given in Child under the title "Captain Care"

Hail master, and whither you will,
And whither ye like it best;
To the castle of Crecynbroghe,
And there we'll take our rest.

I know where is gay castle,
Is built of lime and stone;
Within is a gay lady,
Her lord is rid from home.

They were no sooner at supper set,
Then after said the grace,
Or Captain Care and all his men
Were light about the place.

"Give over thy house, thou lady gay,
And I will make thee a bond,
Tonight thou shall lie within my arms,
Tomorrow be the heir of my land."

"I will not give over my house," she saith,
Neither for lord nor lown,
Nor yet for traitor Captain Care,
The lord of Easter-town.

"Fetch me my pistolet", she said,
"And charge ye well my gun,
That I may shoot yonder bloody butcher
The lord of Easter-town!"

Stiffly upon her wall she stood
And let the pellets flee;
But then she missed the bloody butcher
And yet slew other three.

Then bespoke the youngest son,
That sat on the nurse's knee,
Says "Mother dear, give o'er this house,
For the smoke it smothers me."

"I would give all my gold, my child,
So would I give all my fee,
For one blast of the western wind
To blow the smoke from thee."

"Fie upon thee, John Hamilton,
That ever I paid thy hire,
For thou hast broken my castle wall,
And kindled in the fire!"

But when she saw the fire
Come flaming o'er her head,
She then took up her children three,
Saying, "Babes, we all are dead!"

Then Captain Care he rode away;
He stayed no longer at that tide;
He thought that place it was too warm
So near for to abide.

He called unto his merry-men all
And bade them haste away;
"For we have slain his children three,
All and his lady gay."

When word came to Lord Hamilton,
Lord, in his heart was woe;
Says, "I will find thee Captain Care
Whither thou ride or go!"

Of God,   Of Man,   Of the Divell.

Light o' love

The words used here are attributed to Leonard Gybson and were first printed in 1570 but may have been a reworking of a well-known song as the tune is believed to be much older. Shakespeare refers to it in two plays — "Two Gentlemen of Verona" — Act I Scene II and in "Much Ado About Nothing" — Act III Scene IV.

By force I am fix — ed my fan — cy to write, In — gra — ti — tude wil — leth me not to re — frain. Then blame me not lad — ies al — though I in — dite What light — ly love now __ a — mongst you doth reign. Your trac — es in plac — es with out — ward al — lure — ments, Doth move __ my en — deav — our to be the more plain. Your nic — ings and tic — ings with sun — dry pro — cure — ments, To

pub — lish yon _ light — ie love doth me con — strain.

Deceit is not dainty, it comes at each dish;
And fraud goes a-fishing with friendly looks;
Though friendship is spoil-ed, the silly poor
    fish
That hover and shiver upon your false hooks;
With bait you lay wait to catch here and
    catch there,
Which causes poor fishes their freedom to lose.
Then lout ye and flout ye whereby doth appear
Your lightie love ladies, still cloak-ed with
    gloss.

It was a lover and his lass

Sung by two pages in the play "As You Like It" Act V Scene III, it was composed by Thomas Morley and is really a duet.

It was a lov—er and his lass, with a hey, and a ho, and a hey non-ny—no, And a hey _____ non-ny, non-ny—no, That o'er the green corn-field did pass, In spring—time, in spring—time, in spring—time, The on—ly pret—ty ring—time, When birds do sing, Hey ding-a-ding-a-ding, Hey ding-a-ding-a-ding, Hey ding-a-ding-a-ding, Sweet lov—ers love the spring in spring—time in spring—time, the on — ly pret—ty ring—time, When birds do sing, Hey

ding – a -ding- a- ding. Hey ding- a -ding- a -ding, Hey ding-a-ding- a -ding Sweet

lov – ers love the spring.

This carol they began that hour,
With a hey and a ho and a hey nonino,
And a hey nonne nonino,
How that life was but a flower
In spring time, etc.

Between the acres of the rye,
With a hey, and a ho and a hey nonino,
And a hey nonne nonino,
These pretty country folks would lie,
In spring time, etc.

And therefore take the present time,
With a hey, and a ho and a hey nonino,
And a hey nonne nonino,
For love is crowned with the prime,
In spring time, in spring time, in spring time,
The only pretty ring time,
When birds do sing,
Hey ding a ding a ding,
Hey ding a ding a ding,
Hey ding a ding a ding,
Sweet lovers love the spring.

What shall he have that kill'd the deer

The very short second scene of Act IV in "As You Like It" is devoted almost entirely to this song. As the song was a 'catch' and catches were most popular, and the scene contains a number of foresters who could easily be singers, it seems safe to assume that it might well have been done just the way John Hilton indicated when he printed it in 'Catch as Catches Can' 1652. Adjust this to conform with other catches (rounds). Four people can sing it, each beginning as the previous singer reaches the mark VIII.

What shall he _ have that kill'd the _ deer? His leath — er skin and horns to wear.. Take you no_scorn to wear a _ horn, it was a ____ crest ere thou wast _ born, thy fath—er's fath — er bore __ it And thy fath — er _ wore __ it, the horn, the horn, the lust — y horn is not a thing to laugh to scorn.

Hunt is up, The

Any song intended to arouse in the morning — even a love song — was formerly called a "hunts up" (see Chappell, page 60). Shakespeare so employs it in "Romeo and Juliet" Act III, Scene 5. The tune here is as given by Hullah from "Musick's Delight on the Cithern" 1667, but it resembles closely Chappell's example from Jane Pickering's Lute Book 1615.

The hunt is up! — the hunt is up — and it — is well — nigh day. — And Har — ry our King is gone — hunt — ing to bring — his deer — to bay. ———

The east is bright with morning light,
And darkness it is fled, .
And the merry horn wakes up the morn
To leave his idle bed.

Behold the skies with golden dyes,
Are glowing all around;
The grass is green, and so are the treen
All laughing at the sound.

The horses snort to be at the sport
The dogs are running free
The woods rejoice at the merry noise
Of hey tantara tee ree!

The sun is glad to see us clad
All in our lusty green,
And smiles in the sky as he riseth high
To see and to be seen.

Where griping grief

In "Romeo and Juliet" Act IV Scene 5 Shakespeare indulges in some satirical thrusts at pedantic poety-editors who pick poems to pieces. The lyric under discussion is Richard Edwards' "Where Griping Griefs" printed in "The Paradise of Dainty Devises" 1576.

Where grip - ing grief — the hart would wound

and dole – ful domps the mind — op – presse

There Mus – ick with — her sil – ver sound

50

Am   G   Am   Em   Am   Dm   E   E7   Am

is wont with   spede   to   give re — dresse

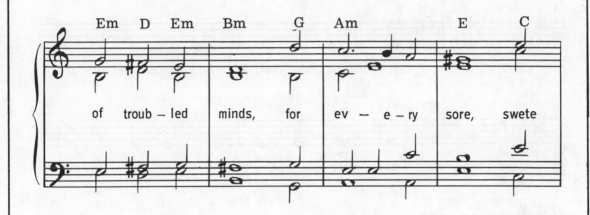

Em   D   Em   Bm   G   Am   E   C

of troub — led   minds,   for   ev — e — ry   sore,   swete

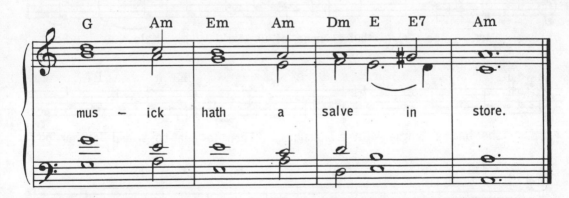

G   Am   Em   Am   Dm   E   E7   Am

mus — ick   hath   a   salve   in   store.

In joy it makes our mirth abound,
In woe it cheers our heavy sprites,
Bestraughte'd heads relief hath found,
By music's pleasant sweet delights:
Our senses all, what shall I say more?
Are subject unto music's lore.

O heavenly, gift, that rules the mind,
Even as the stern doth rule the ship
O music, whom the gods assigned
To comfort man, whom cares would nip!
Since thou both man and beast dost move,
What beast is he, will thee disprove?

Stephano's songs

These snatches of song sung by the sailor Stephano in Act II, Scene 2 of "The Tempest" have not been traced to any earlier ballad nor identified with any tunes other than those provided by Caulfield who says they are given as sung unaccompanied by Mr. John Bannister. The tune sounds as if it might have originated in the 18th century but is apparently traditional in the theatre.

I shall no more to sea, to sea, Here shall I die on — shore! The Mast — er, the Swab — ber, the Boat — swain and I, the Gun — ner and his Mate ___ Lov'd Moll, Meg, Mar — ian and Mar — ge — ry but none of us car'd for Kate. ___ For _ she had a tongue with a tang. Then to sea boys and let her go hang, Then to sea, boys and let her go hang. ___

Thou cans't not hit it

In "Love's Labour Lost" Act IV, Scene 1, Rosalind and Boyet sing this song which is another fragment of an earlier popular ballad. The tune has been preserved in Wm. Ballet's Lute Book but the rest of the words are undiscovered.

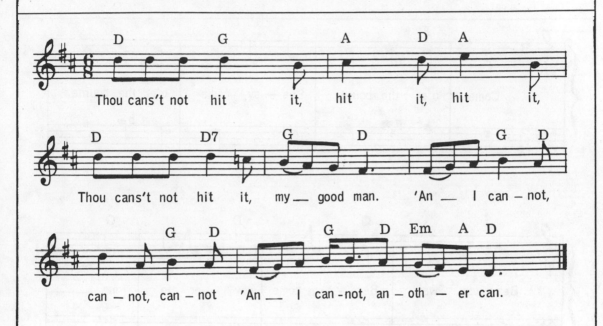

Thou cans't not hit it, hit it, hit it,
Thou cans't not hit it, my good man. 'An I can-not,
can-not, can-not 'An I can-not, an-oth-er can.

Come o'er the bourne, Bessy

In "King Lear", Act III, Scene 6, one of the many references to songs and ballads in that play is made to "Come o'er the Bourne Bessy", which Chappell traces to the beginning of the 16th century. He gives an early version of the words and the later ballad which was undoubtedly current in Shakespeare's time. I have resisted the temptation to make it scan.

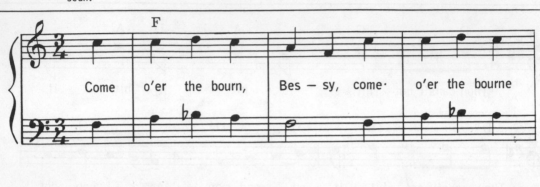

Come o'er the bourn, Bes—sy, come· o'er the bourne

Bes—sy, Sweet Bes—sy come ov—er to me

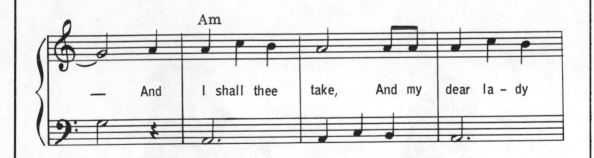

— And I shall thee take, And my dear la—dy

make Be—fore all oth—er that ev—er I see

Bess Answers:

Methinks I hear a voice,
At whom I do rejoice
And answer thee now I shall;
Tell me, I say,
What art thou that bids me come away.
And so earnestly doest me call?

England:

I am the lover fair
Hath chose thee to mine heir,
And my name is Merry England;
Therefore come away,
And make no more delay,
Sweet Bessy, give me thy hand.

Bess:

Here is my hand,
My dear lover, England.
I am thine with both mind and heart;
For ever to endure,
Thou mayest be sure,
Until death us two do depart!

Calino custurame

This is the tune alluded to by Shakespeare in "Henry V" (Act IV Scene 4). It is to be found in the Fitzwilliam Virginal Book. In "A Handful of Pleasant Delites" 1584, the words "Caleno Custurame" are interpolated as a refrain between every two lines of the poem, "When as I view..." They seem to be a perversion of the Irish "Cailin oge a stuir me" or "young girl, my treasure."

When as I view your com - ly grace

Cal - i - no cus - tur - a - me, your gol - den haires, your

an - gel's face, Cal - i - no cus - tur - a - me.

Then how dare I with boldened face,
Caleno custurame;
Presume to crave or wish your grace,
Caleno custurame.

Long life and virtue you possess,
Caleno custurame;
To match those gifts of worthiness,
Caleno custurame.

Carman's whistle, The

Falstaff says of Justice Shallow in "Henry IV", Part II Act 3 that he "sang the tunes he heard the carmen whistle and sware they were his Fancies or his Good-nights." The tune was preserved in the Fitzwilliam Virginal Book and the text somewhat expurgated and abbreviated appears in Chappell.

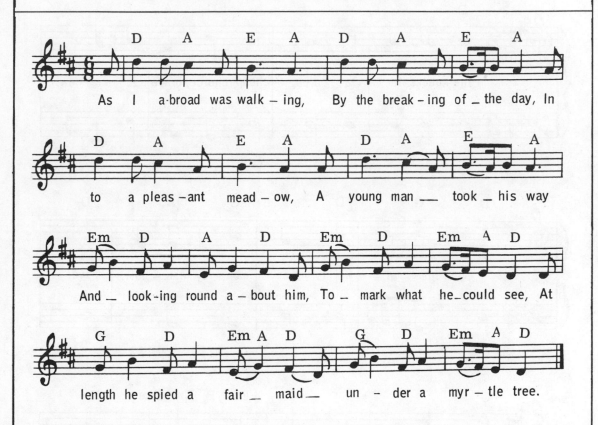

As I a-broad was walk — ing, By the break-ing of — the day, In to a pleas—ant mead—ow, A young man — took — his way And — look-ing round a — bout him, To — mark what he — could see, At length he spied a fair — maid — un - der a myr — tle tree.

So comely was her countenance,
And winning was her air,
As though the goddess Venus
Herself she had been there;
And many a smirking smile she gave
Amongst the leaves so green,
Although she was perceived,
She thought she was not seen.

At length she chang'd her countenance,
And sung a mournful song,
Lamenting her misfortune
She stayed a maid so long;
Sure young men are hard-hearted
And know not what they do,
Or else they look for compliments,
Fair maidens for to woo.

"Why should young virgins pine away
And lose their chiefest prime,
And all for want of sweethearts
To cheer us up in time?"
The young man heard her ditty
And could no longer stay,
But straight unto the damsel
With speed he did away!

When he had played unto her,
One merry note or two,
Then was she so rejoiced
She knew not what to do.
"Oh, God-a-mercy, carman,
Thou art a lively lad;
Thou hast as rare a whistle
As ever carman had."

Fine knacks for ladies

Dowland's 2nd Book of Airs (1600)

Here is a pedlar's song by the greatest songwriter of the period, the mighty John Dowland, a virtuoso performer on the lute and singer of considerable reputation. He was also the first to publish a book of airs (1597). This is a more sophisticated pedlar than Shakespeare's Autolycus but they are of the same mold.

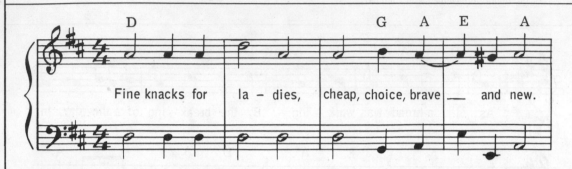

Fine knacks for la – dies, cheap, choice, brave ___ and new.

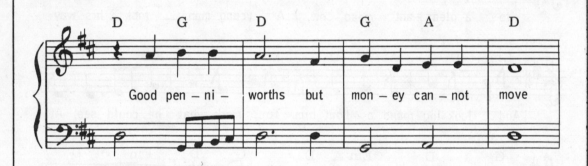

Good pen – ni – worths but mon – ey can – not move

I keep a fair but for the fair to view,

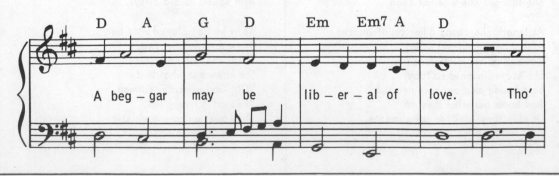

A beg – gar may be lib – er – al of love. Tho'

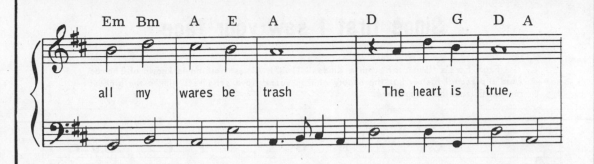

all my   wares be   trash   The heart is   true,

the heart   is   true,   the heart ——— is   true.

*I believe this song to be the expression of his personal feelings directed to his country-
men and his Queen during voluntary exile in Denmark.

Great gifts are guiles and look for gifts again;
My trifles come as treasures from my mind.
It is a precious jewel to be plain;
Sometimes in shell, the Orient's pearls we find.
Of others take a sheaf, of me a grain.

Within this pack, pins, points, laces and gloves,
And divers toys fitting a country fair.
*But in my heart, where duty serves and loves,
Turtles and twins, Court's brood, a heavenly
      pair,
Happy the heart that thinks of no removes.

Since first I saw your face

From Ford's "Music of Sundrie Kindes" (1607). Almost nothing is known of Thomas Ford's personal history but the beauty of this superb love song sets him in the highest rank of Elizabethan composers.

Since first I saw your face I re-solv'd to hon - our and re-nown ye, If now I be dis - dain - ed I wish my heart had nev-er known ye. What! I that lov'd and you that lik'd, shall be be - gin to

wrang – le?　　No, no, no, my heart is fast and can – not

dis – en – tang — le.

If I admire or praise you too much,
That fault you may forgive me.
Or if my hands had strayed a touch,
Then justly might you leave me,
I ask'd you leave, you bade me love,
Is't now a time to chide me?
No, no, no. I'll love you still,
What fortune e'er betide me.

The sun, whose beams most glorious are,
Rejecteth no beholder;
And your sweet beauty, past compare,
Made my poor eyes the holder;
Where beauty moves and wit delights,
And signs of kindness find me,
There, oh there, where'er I go,
I'll leave my heart behind me.

From the fair Lavinian shore

Claimed by Jackson to have been attributed on manuscript evidence to Shakespeare with a setting by John Wilson, it is an early example of the many pseudo-pedlar songs which became popular in the 17th century. (See No. 15 — Lawn as white).

Whether or not these verses are from Shakespeare's hand, it is a good song and typical of the period. A third stanza is found in some early books. This is from the "Academy of Compliments" (1664):

From the fair La-vin-ian _ shore; I your mar-kets come to store Muse not 'tho so far I _ dwell And my wares come here to sell Such is the sac-red hun-ger of gold, ____ Then come to my pack, while I cry, "What d'ye lack, what d'ye buy _ for here it is to be sold.

I have beauty, honour, grace,
Fortune, favour, time and place;
And what else thou wouldst request,
E'en the thing thou lik'st the best.
First let me have a touch of thy gold;
Then come to me lad, thou shalt have
What thy dad never gave,
For here it is to be sold.

Madam, for your wrinkled face,
Here's complexion it to grace,
Which, if your earnest be but small,
It takes away the virtue all;
But if your palms are anointed with gold, —
Then come to my pack, you shall seem
Like a queen of fifteen,
Though you are three score years old.

Tune thy music to thy heart

Tune thy mus - ic to thy heart Sing thy joy with

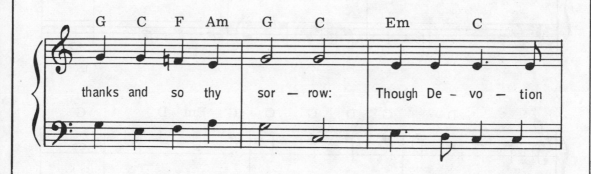

thanks and so thy sor — row: Though De - vo — tion

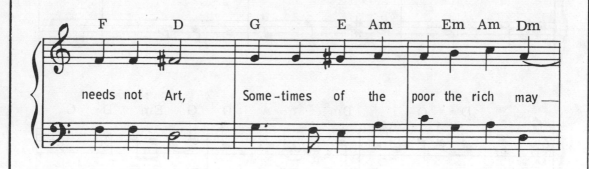

needs not Art, Some-times of the poor the rich may

— bor - row.

Strive not yet for curious ways,
Concord pleaseth more, the less 'tis strained;
Zeal affects not outward praise,
Only strives to show a love unfeigned.

Love can wondrous things effect,
Sweetest sacrifice, all wrath appeasing;
Love the highest doth respect,
Love alone to him is ever pleasing.

Never weather-beaten sail

Thomas Campion, a contemporary of Shakespeare, has been called the most musical of the Elizabethan lyric poets. As a practising physician, he personifies the ideal Elizabethan gentleman, pouring out his creative genius in poetry and music. In his four books of Ayres published from 1601 to 1617, he demonstrated his unique ability to weld words and music in graceful and glorious union.

Nev – er weath – er beat-en sail more will – ing bent to shore

Nev – er tir – ed pil – grim's limbs af – fec – ted slum – ber more

Than my — wear – y — sprite now — longs to fly – out — of — my

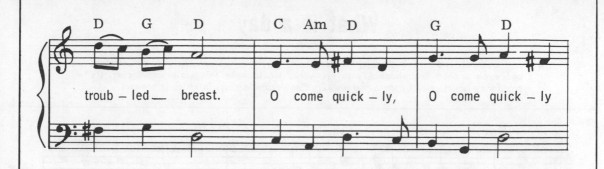

troub – led — breast.   O come quick – ly,   O come quick – ly

O come quick – ly   sweet – est Lord, and — take my — soul to rest.

Ever blooming are the joys of Heav'n's high
    paradise;
Cold age deafs not there our ears, nor vapours
    dims our eyes;
Glory there the sun outshines, whose beams
    the blessed only see;
O come quickly, glorious Lord, and raise my
    sprite to Thee.

What if a day

Chappell and Jackson both site evidence for crediting this song to Thomas Campion, and even a short acquaintance with his works would make this claim convincing. Its popularity is indicated by the numerous 17th Century collections in which it appears.

What if a day or a month or a year, Crown thy de-lights with a thou-sand sweet con-tent – ings, a thou – sand sweet con – tent –ings

may not the change of a night or an hour Cross thy de-lights with as man – y sad tor-ment – ings, as man – y sad tor – ment – ings.

For - tune, hon –our, beau –ty,— youth, are but blos-soms dy – ing

Wan – ton pleas-ures dot-ing – love Are but shad-ows fly – ing

All our joys are but toys, I – dle thoughts de – ceiv – ing

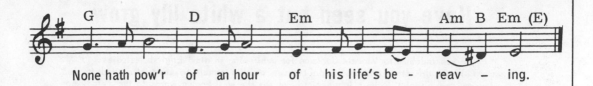

None hath pow'r of an hour of his life's be‑reav—ing.

Th' earth's but a point of the world, and a man
Is but a point of the earth's compar‑ed centre;
Shall then the point of a point be so vain,
As to triumph in a silly point's adventure?
All is hazard that we have.
Here is nothing biding;
Days of pleasure are as streams
Through fair meadows gliding.
Weal or woe, time doth go,
Time hath no returning;
Secret fates guide our states
Both in mirth and mourning.

What if a smile or a beck or a look
Feed thy fond thoughts with many vain
    conceivings?
May not that smile or that beck or that look
Tell thee as well they are all but false
    deceivings?
Why should beauty be so proud
In things of no surmounting?
All her wealth is but a shroud,
Nothing of accounting.
Then in this there's no bliss,
Which is vain and idle,
Beauty's flowers have their hours,
Time doth hold the bridle.

What if the world, with a lure of its wealth,
Raise thy degree to great place of high
    advancing?
May not the world by a check of that wealth,
Bring thee again to as low despis‑ed changing?
While the sun of wealth doth shine,
Thou shalt have friends plenty;
But come want, they repine,
Not one abides of twenty!
Wealth (and friends) holds and ends
As thy fortunes rise and fall;
Up and down, smile and frown,
Certain is no state at all.

Have you seen but a white lily grow

We are indebted to Vincent Jackson for publishing in his "English Melodies" (J. M. Dent 1910) the story and additional verses of this exquisite song attributed to Ben Jonson and lutenist Robert Johnson. I have set the well known words to the melody but given Jackson's verses 1 and 2 as follows:

See the chariot at hand here of love,
Wherein my lady rideth!
Each that draws is a swan or a dove;
And well the car love guideth —
As she goes, all hearts do duty
Unto her beauty;
And enamour'd do wish, so they might
But enjoy such a sight,
That they still were to run by her side
Thro' swords, thro' seas, whither she would
    glide.

Do but look on her eyes, they do light
All that love's world compriseth!
Do but look on her hair, it is bright
As love's star when it riseth!
Do but mark, her forehead's smoother
Than words that soothe her.
And from her arched brows such a grace
Sheds itself thro' the face,
As alone there triumphs to the life
All the gain, all the good of the elements'
    strife.

Ah! the sighs that come fro' the heart

From the appendix to the King's (Henry VIII) MSS in the British Museum where there is also another setting directly attributed to Wm. Cornyshe (1480–1524) whom Gibbon describes as 'admirable poet, musician and occasional jailbird' at the court of Henry VIII.

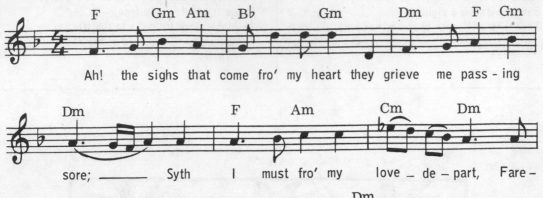

Ah! the sighs that come fro' my heart they grieve me pass - ing

sore; —— Syth I must fro' my love _ de - part, Fare -

well my joy for - ev - er - more. ———

Oft to me with her goodly face,
She was wont to cast an eye;
And now absence to me in place!
Alas! for woe I die, I die.

I was wont her to behold,
And take in armes twain;
And now with syghes manifold,
Farewell my joy and welcome pain!

Ah, me think that should I yet,
As would to God that I might;
There would no joys compare with it
Unto my heart, to make it light.

Ah! the syghes that come fro' my heart,
They grieve me passing sore;
Syth I must fro' my love depart,
Farewell my joye for ever more.

[Queen Katharine.]

[Anne Bullen.]

70

Pastime with good company

Chappell claims the words and tune to be the work of King Henry VIII. They were found at the British Museum in a manuscript of the early part of the 16th century. While the tune does not seem to be too characteristic of that period, the verses seem quite consistent with what we know of Henry's philosophy.

Youth will needs have dalliance,
Of good or ill some pastance;
Company me thinketh the best
All thoughts and Fantasies to digest.
For idleness
Is chief mistress
Of vices all;
Then who can say
But pass the day
Is best of all?

Company with honesty
Is virtue; and vice to flee.
Company is good or ill,
But every man hath his free will.
The best I sue,
The worst eschew;
My mind shall be
Virtue to use,
Vice to refuse,
I shall use me.

Agincourt song, The

An early example (probably 15th century) of a popular song praising a great English victory. It is early enough that part of the lyric or refrain is in Latin. The whole song with the tune to which it was sung may be found in Percy's Reliques Book IV, where it was copied from a manuscript in the Pepys collection.

Our King went forth to Nor-man - dy, with
grace — and might — of — chiv-al - ry; The God for
him — wrought mar - v'lous - ly, Where — fore Eng — land may
call and cry, De — — o gra - ti - as, De -
o gra - ti - as, An - gli - — a red - de pro
vic - to - — ri - a.

Now gracious God he save our king,
His people and all his well willing,
Give him good life and good ending,
That we with mirth may safely sing.

Cold's the wind and wet's the rain

(The Cobbler's Jig)

Convivial song to the tune designated in the "Dancing Master" as "The Cobbler's Jig". Although the text used here makes no reference whatever to the cobbler, it might safely be assumed that he enjoyed a bowl as much as the butcher, the baker or the candlestick maker.

Cold's the wind and wet's the rain; St. Hugh be our good speed! Ill is the weath-er that bring—eth no gain, Nor helps good hearts in need. Hey down, a—down, hey — down a—down, hey — der—ry der—ry down a—down; — Ho! well done, To me let come, Ring com—pass, gen—tle joy.

Troll the bowl, the nut-brown bowl,
And here, kind mate, to thee!
Let's sing a dirge for Saint Hugh's soul,
And drown it merrily.

All in a garden green

This song has an opening line common to many songs of the period, but the poem is married by Chappell to a popular Country Dance tune called "Gathering Peascods" which is noted in William Ballet's Lute book of 1594.

All in a gar – den green Two lov – ers sat at ease, As they could scarce be senn a – mong, a – mong the leaf – y trees. They long had lov'd y'-fore. And no long – er than tru – ly In that time — of the year, — in that time — of the year com — eth 'twixt May— and Ju – ly.

Quoth he, "Most lovely maid,
My troth shall aye endure,
And be not thou afraid
But rest thee still secure.
That I will love thee long
As life in me shall last,
Now I am young and strong,
And when my youth is past.

She listed to his song,
And heard it with a smile,
And innocent as she was young
She dreamed not of guile.
No guile he meant, I ween,
For he was true as steel,
As was thereafter seen
When she made him her weal.

Quoth John to Joan

(WOLSEY'S WILD)

A popular dance tune which appeared in lute and virginal books. The tune is taken from the Fitzwilliam book as the text fits it without repetition.

Quoth John to Joan, — "Wilt thou — have me? I
prith — ee now wilt and I'se mar — ry with thee. My cow, — my calf, my
horse, — my rents, And all — my lands and ten — e -ments,
Chorus O say, my Joan will not that do. I
can — not come ev' — ry day to woo.

I've corn and hay in the barn hard by,
And three fat hogs pent up in the sty;
I have a mare and she is coal-black,
I ride on her tail to save her back.

I have a cheese upon the shelf,
And I cannot eat it all myself;
I've three good marks that lie in a rag,
In the nook of the chimney instead of a bag.

To marry I would have thy consent,
But faith, I never could compliment;
I can say nought but 'hoy, gee ho!'
Words that belong to the cart and the plough.

Who hath his fancy pleas'd

Attributed to Sir Philip Sidney who quite obviously composed his lines to be sung to the tune "Wilhelmus van Nassauen" which has remained the Dutch national anthem to the present day. A full account is given in Gibbon, p. 70.

Who hath his fan-cy— pleas'd with— fruits of hap-py sight, Let here his eyes be— rais'd on— nat-ure's sweet-est light. A— light which doth dis-sev-er and yet u-nite the eyes. A light —which dy—ing nev-er is 'cause the look—er dies.

She never dies, but lasteth
In life of lover's heart;
He ever dies that wasteth
In love his chiefest part.
Thus in her life still guarded
In never dying faith,
Thus is his death rewarded,
Since she lives in his death.

Look then and die. The pleasure
Doth answer well the pain.
Small loss of mortal treasure,
Who may immortal gain.
Immortal be her graces,
Immortal is her mind;
They fit for heavenly places,
This heaven in it doth bind.

Spanish Lady, The

Not to be confused with the Irish folk song of the same name nor the sea-shanty "Spanish Ladies", but all of them probably have their origin in the contact of British soldiers and sailors with the ladies of Spain during the expeditions against the Spaniards in the latter part of Queen Elizabeth's reign. The Englishman in the song has been variously identified as being Sir Richard Levison, Sir John Bolle and a gentleman of the Popham family. Anyway, the sixteen verse ballad of which we have used only four verses, is reproduced in Percy's Reliques where it was copied from an ancient black-letter copy. The tune is in the Skene manuscript which is dated about 1615.

Will you hear a Span-ish la—dy, How she woo'd an Eng—lish man? Gar—ments rare and rich as may—be Deck'd with Jew—els she had on. Of a come-ly coun-ten-ance and grace was she, And by birth and par-ent-age of high de—gree.

But at last there came commandment
For to set the ladies free,
With their jewels still adorn-ed,
None to do them injury.
Then said this lady mild, "Full woe is me,
O, let me sustain this kind captivity."

Courteous lady, leave this fancy,
Here comes all that breeds the strife,
I in England have already
A sweet woman to my wife.
I'll not falsify my vow for gold and gain,
Nor for all the fairest dames that live in Spain.

Then commend me to thy lady,
Bear to her this chain of gold,
And these bracelets for a token,
Grieving that I was so bold.
See, my jewels in like sort take thou with thee,
They are fitting for thy wife, but not for me.

High Barbary

Cecil Sharp claims this is an old broadside sea song probably written in the latter part of the sixteenth century. He also points out that it was quoted in a play "The Two Noble Kinsmen" written by Johnn Fletcher and William Shakespeare.

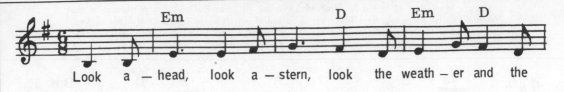

Look a—head, look a—stern, look the weath—er and the

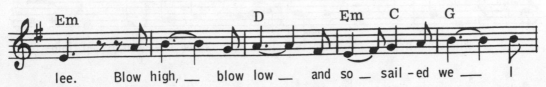

lee. Blow high, __ blow low __ and so __ sail—ed we __ I

see a wreck to wind—ward and__ a loft—y ship to lee, A—

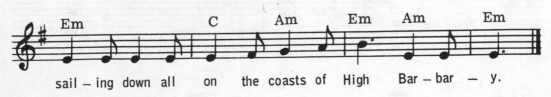

sail—ing down all on the coasts of High Bar—bar—y.

O are you a pirate or man o'war, cried we?
Blow high! blow low! and so sailed we
O no! I'm not a pirate, but a man o'war, cried he,
A sailing down all on the coasts of High
  Barbary.

Then back up your topsails and heave your
  vessel to,
Blow high! blow low! and so sailed we.
For we have got some letters to be carried
  home by you.
A-sailing down all on the coasts of High
  Barbary.

We'll be back up our topsails and heave our
  vessel to;
Blow high! blow low: and so sailed we.
But only in some harbour and along the side
  of you.
A-sailing down all on the coasts of High
  Barbary.

For broadside, for broadside, they fought all on
  the main;
Blow high! blow low! and so sailed we.
Until at last the frigate shot the pirate's
  mast away.
A-sailing down all on the coasts of High
  Barbary.

For quarters! for quarters! the saucy pirate cried.
Blow high! blow low! and so sailed we.
The quarters that we showed them was to sink
  them in the tide.
A-sailing down all on the coasts of High
  Barbary.

With cutlass and gun O we fought for hours three;
Blow high! blow low! and so sailed we.
The ship it was their coffin, and their grave it
  was the sea.
A-sailing down all on the coasts of High
  Barbary.

But O! it was a cruel sight, and grieved us full
    sore,
Blow high! blow low! and so sailed we.
To see them all a-drowning as they tried to
    swim to shore.
A-sailing down all on the coasts of High
    Barbary.

King Lear and his three daughters

As the date of this ballad is not known, it is impossible to determine whether Shakespeare's play was based on the ballad or vice-versa. The ballad is very long (23 double stanzas are given in Percy) but is performed in an abbreviated version (15 verses) by Ewan McColl on Folkways F.W. 3443 to the tune "Flying Fame".

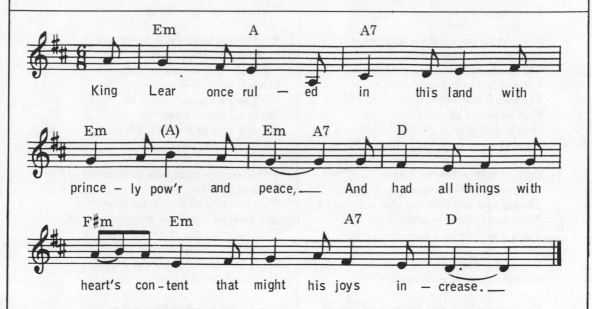

King Lear once rul — ed in this land with prince — ly pow'r and peace, __ And had all things with heart's con — tent that might his joys in — crease. __

King Leir once ruled in this land
With princely power and peace,
And had all things with hearts content,
That might his joys increase.
Amongst those things that nature gave,
Three daughters fair had he,
So princely seeming beautiful,
As fairer could not be.

So on a time it pleas'd the king
A question thus to move,
Which of his daughters to his grace
Could shew the dearest love:
"For to my age you bring content,"
Quoth her, "then let me hear,
Which of you three in plighted troth
The kindest will appear."

To whom the eldest thus began:
"Dear father, mind," quoth she,
"Before your face, to do you good,
My blood shall render'd be.
And for your sake my bleeding heart
Shall here be cut in twain,
Ere that I see your reverend age
The smallest grief sustain."

"And so will I," the second said;
"Dear father, for your sake,
The worst of all extremities
I'll gently undertake:
And serve your highness night and day
With diligence and love;
That sweet content and quietness
Discomforts may remove."

"In doing so, you glad my soul,"
The aged king reply'd;
"But what sayst thou, my youngest girl,
How is thy love ally'd?"
"My love (quoth young Cordelia then),
"Which to your grace I owe,
Shall be the duty of a child,
And that is all I'll show."

"And wilt thou shew no more," quoth he,
"Than doth thy duty bind?
I well perceive thy love is small,
When as no more I find.
Henceforth I banish thee my court;
Thou art no child of mine;
Nor any part of this my realm
By favour shall be thine.

"Thy elder sisters loves are more
Than well I can demand;
To whom I equally bestow
My kingdome and my land,
My pompal state and all my goods,
That lovingly I may
With those thy sisters be maintain'd
Until my dying day."

Thus flattering speeches won renown,
By these two sisters here;
The third had causeless banishment,
Yet was her love more dear.
For poor Cordelia patiently
Went wandring up and down,
Unhelp'd, unpity'd, gentle maid,
Through many an English town:

Until at last in famous France
She gentler fortunes found;
Though poor and bare, yet she was deem'd
The fairest on the ground:
Where when the king her virtues heard,
And this fair lady seen,
With full consent of all his court
He made his wife and queen.

Her father, old King Leir, this while
With his two daughters staid;
Forgetful of their promis'd loves,
Full soon the same decay'd;
And living in Queen Ragan's court,
The eldest of the twain,
She took from him his chiefest means,
And most of all his train.

For whereas twenty men were wont
To wait with bended knee,
She gave allowance but to ten,
And after scarce to three,
Nay, one she thought too much for him;
So took she all away,
In hope that in her court, good king,
He would no longer stay.

"Am I rewarded thus," quoth he,
"In giving all I have
Unto my children, and to beg
For what I lately gave?
I'll go unto my Gonorell:
My second child, I know,
Will be more kind and pitiful,
And will relieve my woe."

Full fast he hies then to her court;
Where when she heard his moan,
Return'd him answer, that she griev'd
That all his means were gone,
But no way could relieve his wants;
Yet if that he would stay
Within her kitchen, he should have
What scullions gave away.

When he had heard, with bitter tears,
He made his answer then;
"In what I did, let me be made
Example to all men,
I will return again," quoth he,
"Unto my Ragan's court;
She will not use me thus, I hope,
But in a kinder sort."

Where when he came, she gave command
To drive him thence away:
When he was well within her court,
(She said) he would not stay.
Thus twixt his daughters for relief
He wandred up and down,
Being glad to feed on beggars food,
That lately wore a crown.

And calling to remembrance then
His youngest daughters words,
That said, the duty of a child
Was all that love affords —
But doubting to repair to her,
Whom he had banish'd so,
Grew frantic mad; for in his mind
He bore the wounds of woe.

Which made him rend his milk-white locks
And tresses from his head,
And all with blood bestain his cheeks,
With age and honour spread.
To hills and woods and watry founts,
He made his hourly moan,
Till hills and woods and senseless things
Did seem to sigh and groan.

Even thus possest with discontents,
He passed o're to France,
In hopes from fair Cordelia there
To find some gentler chance.
Most virtuous dame! which, when she heard
Of this her father's grief,
As duty bound, she quickly sent
Him comfort and relief.

And by a train of noble peers,
In brave and gallant sort,
She gave in charge he should be brought
To Aganippus' court;
Whose royal king, with noble mind,
So freely gave consent
To muster up his knights at arms,
To fame and courage bent.

And so to England came with speed,
To repossesse King Leir,
And drive his daughters from their thrones
By his Cordelia dear.
Where she, true-hearted, noble queen,
Was in the battel slain;
Yet he, good king, in his old days,
Possest his crown again.

But when he heard Cordelia's death,
Who died indeed for love
Of her dear father, in whose cause
She did this battle move,
He swooning fell upon her breast,
From whence he never parted;
But on her bossom left his life
That was so truly hearted.

When Samson was a tall young man

One of the many ballads sung to the "Spanish Pavan" which was a very popular dance and ballad tune during the reign of Elizabeth and James II as attested by many references in writings of the period and its appearance in numerous lute books. The text is in Pepys i, 32. (Abbreviated from the 21 stanza ballad, "A most excellent and famous ditty of Samson, judge of Israel......"

When Sam-son was a tall young man, His pow'r and strength in-creas — ed then, And in the host and tribe of Dan The Lord did bless him al — way. It chanc — ed so up — on a day. As _ he was walk — ing on his way, He saw a maid — en fresh and gay In Tim -nath, in _ Tim - nath.

Then on Delilah fair and bright,
Did Samson set his whole delight,
Whom he did love both day and night,
   Which wrought his overthrow;
For she with sweet words did entreat
That for her sake he would repeat
Wherein his strength, that was so great,
   Consisted.

At length unto his bitter fall,
And through her suit, which was not small,
He did not let to show her all
   The secrets of his heart:
If that my hair be cut, quoth he,
Which now so fair and long you see,
Like other men then shall I be
   In weakness.

Then through deceit which was so deep,
She lulled Samson fast asleep,
A man she call'd, which she did keep,
  To cut off all his hair;
Then did she call his hateful foes,
E'er Samson from her lap arose,
Who could not then withstand their blows,
  For weakness.

To bind him fast they did devise,
Then did they put out both his eyes,
In prison woefully he lies,
  And there he grinds the mill;
But God remembered all his pain,
And did restore his strength again,
Although that bound he did remain
  In prison.

The Phillistines now were glad of this,
For joy they made a feast (I wiss),
And all their princes did not miss
  To come unto the same:
And being merry bent that day,
For Samson they did send straightway,
That they might laugh to see him play
  Among them.

Then to the house was Samson led,
And when he had their fancies fed,
He pluck'd the house upon their head,
  And down they tumbl'd all;
So that with grief and deadly pain,
Three thousand persons there were slain,
Thus Samson then with all his train
  Was brained.

Go from my window

This song has apparently survived in oral tradition since Shakespeare's time and it was mighty popular then. Baring-Gould takes over a page and a half in "Songs of the West" to detail its fascinating history. Although not used by Shakespeare, it was quoted in three of Fletcher's plays.

The second verse quoted by Chappell from the "Knight of the Burning Pestle" does not fit this tune, but fits beautifully "Tomorrow is St. Valentine's Day." However, to adapt it and the other traditional verses to this song is a very simple matter. Just alter the third and fourth lines of each stanza.

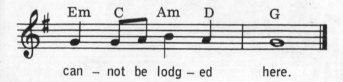

Go from my window love, go,
Go from my window my dear;
The wind is in the west
And the cuckoo's in his nest,
You cannot be lodged here.

Go from my window love, go
Go from my window my dear;
The devil's in the man,
And he cannot understand
That he cannot be lodged here.

Three ravens, The

From Thomas Ravenscroft's famous collection of popular songs titled "Melismata" dated 1611. The songs in this book were generally considered to be much older. Versions of a song about three crows are still current among folk singers to-day.

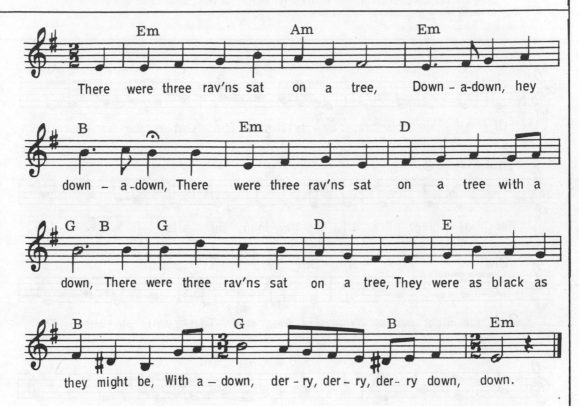

There were three rav'ns sat on a tree, Down – a-down, hey down – a-down, There were three rav'ns sat on a tree with a down, There were three rav'ns sat on a tree, They were as black as they might be, With a – down, der – ry, der – ry, der – ry down, down.

Then one of them said to his mate,
"Where shall we our breakfast take?"

"Down in yonder greene field
There lies a knight slain under his shield."

"His hounds they lie down at his feet,
So well they can their master keep."

"His hawks they fly so eagerly,
There's no fowle dare come him nigh".

Down there comes a fallow doe,
As great with young as she might go.

She lift up his bloody head,
And kissed his wound that were so red.

She got him up upon her back,
And carried him to an earthen lake.

She buried him before the prime,
She was dead herself ere evensong time.

God send every gentleman
Such hawks, such hounds and such a leman.
With a down, derry derry derry down, down.

Of all the birds

Merrythought, in "The Knight of the Burning Pestle," sings three snatches of song from Pammelia and this one from Deuteromelia ("Sing we now merrily" will be found in Noah Greenberg's Elizabethan Song Book). Long points out the similarity between this song and the songs of Spring and Winter at the end of "Love's Labour Lost" and even tries to match the winter stanzas to this tune.

Of all the birds that ev-er I see, The Owl is the fair-est in her de-gree, For all the day long she sits in a tree, And when the night comes a-way flies she. To whit, to whoo, To whom drinks thou? Sir knave to you, — This song is well sung. I make you a vow, And he is a knave that drink-eth now. Nose, Nose, jol-ly red nose, and who gave thee that jol-ly red nose?

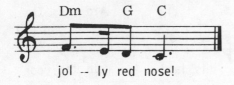

Cin – na – mon, gin – ger, nut--meg and cloves, And that gave me my

jol -- ly red nose!

A
PLEASANT
Conceited Comedie
CALLED,
Loues labors loft.

As it was prefented before her Highnes
this laft Chriftmas.

Newly corrected and augmented
By W. Shakeſpere.

Imprinted at London by W.W.
for Cutbert Burby.
1598.

Who liveth so merry

An early example from Ravenscroft's Deuteromelia of a song built on occupations. Many more such songs are found in "Pills to Purge Melancholy".

Who liv—eth so mer—ry in all _ this land As doth the poor wid—ow that sel—leth the sand? And ev—er she sing—eth as I can guess, "Will you buy an—y sand, an—y sand _ Mis—tress?

The broom-man maketh his living most sweet,
With carrying of brooms from street to street;
Who would desire a pleasanter thing
Than all the day long doing nothing but sing?

The chimney sweeper all the long day,
He singeth and sweepeth the soot away,
Yet when he comes home, although he be
    weary,
With his sweet wife he maketh himself full
    merry.

The cobbler he sits cobbling till noon,
And cobbleth his shoes till they be done;
Yet doth he not fear, and so doth say,
For he knows his work will soon decay.

The serving man waiteth from street to street,
With blowing his nails and beating his feet;
And serveth for forty shillings a year,
How can he be merry and make good cheer?

Who liveth so merry and maketh such sport,
As those that be of the poorest sort?
The poorest sort, wheresoever they be
They gather together by one two and three;
And every man will spend his penny,
What makes such a show among a great many.

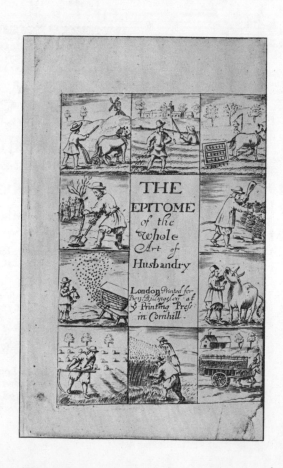

Martin said to his man

One of the Freemen's Songs to three voices in Deuteromelia 1609. In the life of Sir Peter Carew by John Vowell, he says "For the King himself (Henry VIII) being much delighted to sing, and Sir Peter Carew having a pleasant voice, the King would often use him to sing with him certain songs they call "Freemen Songs". This one was licensed in 1588 and is obviously in the line of such traditional songs of exaggeration as "Tom-a-lyn", "Paddy Backwards", and "I was born 1000 years ago."

Mar – tin said to his man, Fie, man, fie, O

Mar – tin said to his man, Who's the fool now? Mar – tin said to his man,

Fill thou the cup and I the can. Thou hast well drunk – en, man;

who's the fool now?

I see a man in the moon,
Fie, man, fie;
I see a man in the moon,
Who's the fool now?
I see a man in the moon
Clouting of St. Peter's shoon,
Thou has well drunken man,
Who's the fool now?

I see a hare chase a hound
Twenty miles above the ground.

I see a goose ring a hog
And a snail that did bite a dog.

I see a mouse catch a cat,
And the cheese to eat the rat.

We be three poor mariners

Another strong tune from Deuteromelia, with some phrases resembling parts of "All in a garden green" or "Gathering Peacods," a dance tune in "The Dancing Master". There would seem to be no doubt that it served both as a song and tune for dancing, and sailors were noted for their ability to dance.

We be three poor mar-in-ers, New - ly _ come from the
seas; We spend our lives in jeo-par-dy,—While oth-ers live in
ease. *Chorus* Shall we go dance the round, the round, the round, Shall
we _ go dance the round, the round, the round, And he that is a
bul - ly boy,—Come pledge me on_ this ground, a ground, a ground.

We care not for those martial men
That do our states disdain;
But we care for those merchant men
Who do our states maintain;
To them we dance this round, around, around;
To them we dance this round, around, around;
And he that is a bully boy,
Come pledge me on this ground, aground,
    aground.

We be soldiers three

Another of the Freemen's Songs to Three Voices in Deuteromelia. "Romeo and Juliet," Act II Scene 4, refers to "these pardonnez-mois who stand so much on the new form". Dr. Johnson says "Pardonnez moi became the language of doubt or hesitation among men of the sword, when the point of honour was grown so delicate that no other mode of contradiction would be endured."

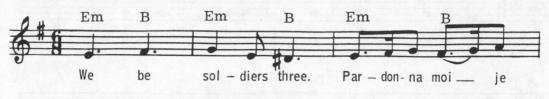

We be sol-diers three. Par—don-na moi —— je

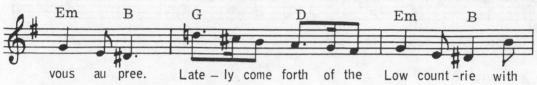

vous au pree. Late—ly come forth of the Low count-rie with

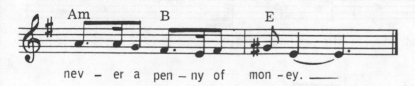

nev—er a pen—ny of mon—ey. ——

Here good fellow, I drink to thee,
Pardon-a-moy, je vous au pree.
To all good fellows wherever they be,
With never a penny of money.

And he that will not pledge me this,
Pardon-a-moy, je vous au pree.
Pays for the shot whatever it is,
With never a penny of money.

Charge it again boy, charge it again,
Pardon-a-moy, je vous au pree.
As long as there is any ink in the pen,
With never a penny of money.

Willy, prithee go to bed

This song appears twice in Deuteromelia (1609) to the tune of "Trenchmore". As the tune is much better than either version of the words, I have combined the two songs in one, retaining the hunting yodel, and adding a concluding line of my own.

Wil — ly, prith — ee go to bed, For thou wilt have a
drow — sy head; To — mor — row we must a hunt — ing
And be times be stir — ring. With a hey trol — ly
lol — ly lol — ly — ly lol - ly - ly lol - ly - ly lol - ly - ly lol - ly - ly
Hey — ho tro — lo — lo — lol — ly — ly — lo. _____

Tomorrow the fox will come to town
I must invite all the neighbours down
To hallo the fox out of the hall
And cry as loud as they can call
With a hey, etc.

He'll steal the cock out from his flock
He'll steal the hen out of her pen
He'll steal the duck out of the brook
And steal the lamb e'en from his dam
With a hey, etc.

But it is like to be fair weather,
Couple all my hounds together;
Couple Finch with old black Troll,
Let Chanter go with young Jumbole.
With a hey, etc.

For chanter opens very well,
But merry she doth hear the hell;
So prick the path and wind the horn,
We'll hunt the fox at break of morn.

Now Robin lend to me thy bow

From Ravenscroft's Pammelia, or "Pleasant Roundelais and Delightful Catches".

1. Now Rob-in lend ——— to me thy bow 2.

2. Sweet Rob - in lend thy bow to me 3.

3. For I must now a – hunt – ing to my la-dy go 4.

4. With my sweet La – – – dy. 1.

Cryes of London

The street cries of the boot-black, the cooper and the chimney sweep as given by Deering in his "Humerous Fancy" (1610). The chimney sweep's song is also used in Orlando Gibbon's work, suggesting that they were based on the traditional songs in current use. The cooper's song uses the first two lines of the tune "Heart's ease".

Sweep, chim — ney sweep, sweep, chim — ney sweep

Sweep, chim — ney mis — tress — sweep with a hoop der — ry, der — ry, der — ry

sweep. From the bot — tom to the top, sweep chim — ney

sweep! There shall no soot fall in your por — ridge pot with a

hoop der — ry, der — ry, der — ry sweep!

Buy an — y black, buy an — y black, here cries one dare bold — ly —

crack, he car — ries that u — pon his back Will make old shoes look ve — ry

black, will ye buy ———— an – y black – ing maids?

A coop – er I am and have been long and hoop – ing

is my trade. And mar – ried I am to as

pret – ty a wench as ev – er God hath made!

Have ye work for a coop — er?

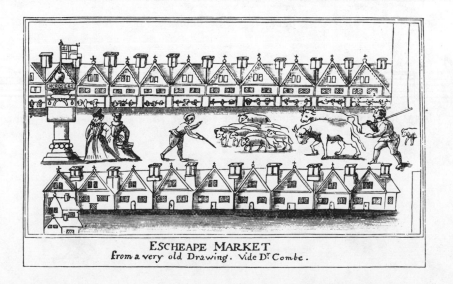

ESCHEAPE MARKET
from a very old Drawing. Vide Dr Combe.

New oysters

A round based on the street cries. From Ravenscroft's "Pammelia and other Rounds & Catches".

1. New oys — ters, New

2. at a groat a peck, at a

3. fetch us bread and wine that we may eat, let us

1. oys — ters. New wale — fleet

2. groat a peck, each oys — ter

3. lose no time with such good meat, a ban — quet for ___

98

1. oys — ters. 2.

2. worth two pence 3.

3. — a prince. 1.

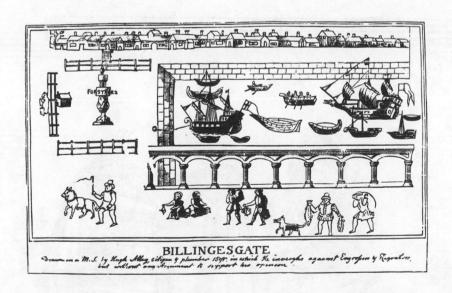

BILLINGESGATE

Drawn in a M.S. by Hugh Alley, citizen & plumber 1598; in which he inveighs against Engrosers & Regraters but without any Argument to support his opinion.

Chairs to mend

Another round based on the street cries common in Shakespeare's time. It is attributed in the Oxford Song Book to Dr. Hayes, Professor of Music, at Oxford in 1776.

1. Chairs to mend, old chairs to mend; Rush or cane bot-tom, old chairs to mend! Old chairs to mend!

2. New mack — er — el, New mack — er — el, Who'll buy new mack — er — el! New mack — er — el!

3. Old rags, an — y old rags, Take mon — ey for your old rags an — y hare skins or rab — bit skins?

Hey ho, nobody at home

Another of the delightful catches from Pammelia sung by Merrythought in Act IV, Scene 5 of "The Knight of the Burning Pestle".

1. Hey, ho!
2. No — bod — y at home
3. Meat nor drink nor
4. mon — ey have I none
5. yet will I be mer — ry.

Loath to depart

The "Auld Lang Syne" of the Elizabethan period, it was sufficiently common to be mentioned in several works including Beaumont and Fletcher's "Wit at Several Weapons" and others; see Chappell, or as a round from Deuteromelia for four voices.

Sing with thy mouth, sing with thy heart,

Like faith — ful friends sing loath to de — part:

Tho' friends to — geth — er may not al — ways re — main, yet

loath to de — part sing once a — gain.

1. Sing with thy mouth, sing with ___ thy heart,

2. Like faith — ful friends sing loath to de — part

3. Though friends to — geth — er may not al — ways re — main, yet

loath   to de – part   sing   once   a – gain.

BIBLIOGRAPHY

Caulfield, John — Vocal Music to Shakespeare's Plays Vol. II (engraved from original mss, and early printed copies)

Bantock, Granville — One Hundred Songs of England (Ditson 1914)

Chappell, W. — Old English Popular Music (Wooldridge 1893)

Gibbon, John Murray — Melody and the Lyric (Dent 1930)

Long, J. H. — Shakespeare's Use of Music, Vols. I & II University of Florida Press 1955 & 1961

Naylor, E. W. — Shakespeare and Music (Dent 1896 & rev. ed. 1931) Shakespeare Music (Curwen 1912)

Hullah, John — The Song Book (MacMillan & Co. 1866)

Hubler, Edward — Shakespeare's Songs and Poems (McGraw, Hill 1959)

Bridge, Sir Frederick — Shakespearean Music in the Plays and Early Operas (Dent 1923)

Vincent, Charles — Fifty Shakespeare Songs (Ditson 1905)

Keel, Frederick — Music in the Time of Queen Elizabeth (Private 1914)

Percy, Thomas (Lord Bishop of Dromore) — Reliques of Ancient English Poetry (Vols. 1 & 2, Geo. Bell & Sons 1876)

Sharp, Cecil — One Hundred English Folk Songs (Ditson 1916)

Baring-Gould, Rev. S. — English Minstrelsie (8 Volumes, No date)

Jackson, Vincent — English Melodies from the 13th to 18th Century (Dent 1910)